INCREASE PRODUCTIVITY AND PROFITABILITY
WITH PROVEN SPRAY EQUIPMENT STRATEGIES
FOR PURCHASING, USAGE AND MAINTENANCE.

STOP
Spraying Money
Down *the* Drain

A MUST-READ
REFERENCE GUIDE
for PEST
MANAGEMENT
and LAWN CARE
PROFESSIONALS

ANDREW GREESS

Printed in the United States of America
0985858931

ISBN 978-0-9858589-3-3

Published by North Coast Media, LLC,
1360 East 9Th St., Suite 1070, Cleveland, OH 44114

North Coast Media, LLC
is a U.S. business information company
that publishes magazines and journals,
produces expositions and conferences,
and provides a wide range of
marketing services.

TABLE OF CONTENTS

Part 1   **Spray Equipment Strategy:**   **10 - 37**
             Plan Before You Buy
   A.   Common spray equipment purchasing errors
   B.   Company strategy should drive spray
             equipment selection
   C.   Strategic questions to consider when evaluating
             new spray equipment
   D.   Spray equipment should support the company brand
   E.   Protecting and retaining employees: Is your spray
             equipment up to the challenge?
   F.   Purchase price is the tip of the iceberg
   G.   Spray equipment selection: Start here
   H.   Equipment standardization: It works for
             Southwest Airlines; it will work for you
   I.   Spray equipment and integrated pest management (IPM)

Part 2   **Power Spray Components**   **38 - 83**
   A.   Start with the tank
   B.   Spray hose – too much isn't enough
   C.   Hose reels
   D.   Power sprayer motor
   E.   Power sprayer pump: The heart of the system
   F.   Spray guns and tools
   G.   Spray tips
   H.   Other components: Supply hoses, fittings, clamps,
             valves and quick disconnects
   I.   Agitation
   J.   Tank pickup line
   K.   Filtration: The most important idea to boost
             sprayer productivity
   L.   Storage: make sure to leave room
   M.   The truck and power spray equipment

Part 3 **Power Spray Equipment Design** **84 - 91**
       and Layout
 A. Skid vs. component vs. trailer mount
 B. Spray equipment: Design for access

Part 4 **Manual Sprayers: Start with the** **92 - 97**
       Right Equipment
 A. Selection: Start with the right equipment
 B. Use: Smart use extends product life
 C. Maintenance: Waiting for problems is expensive

Part 5 **Spray Equipment Policies for Safety,** **98 - 131**
       Savings and Productivity
 A. Safety: Not just a good idea, it's a sound investment
 B. Proper valving prevents spills and other problems
 C. Preventive maintenance isn't optional
 D. Clean it out to prevent problems
 E. Preflight checklist: Save time, save money, serve customers
 F. Spray equipment: Ignoring problems isn't a strategy
 G. Pressure issues that will ruin the day
 H. Emergency repair kits: Problems will occur, so be ready
 I. Back up critical spray equipment
 J. Prevent freeze damage
 K. Use spray equipment properly
 L. Equipment inspections: Trust but verify
 M. Policies and procedures

Appendix **132 - 143**
 A. Top 5 year-end equipment tips
 B. Top 10 spray equipment productivity tips
 C. Quality spray tips
   1. Buying a new power sprayer
   2. Tank tips
   3. Spray hose tips
   4. Hose reel tips
   5. Spray pump tips
   6. Backpack and hand sprayer tips
 D. Preflight checklist

Definitions Spray Equipment Definitions **144 - 145**

This book is dedicated to the loving memory of my favorite people, who I miss every day:

- *Stanley and Laura Greess*
- *Lillian Hollander*
- *Isadore and Lillian Steinberg*

WHY I WROTE THIS BOOK

As the president of a spray equipment company (Quality Equipment & Spray, www.qspray.com) for more than a dozen years, I'm constantly surprised by the huge number and variety of spray equipment problems. It's amazing so many of these problems are avoidable. Here are some of the problems:

- buying the wrong equipment;
- buying solely on price;
- using equipment incorrectly;
- using equipment for applications it wasn't designed for;
- abusing equipment;
- not cleaning equipment;
- ignoring warning signs that lead to equipment problems;
- not securing equipment in the vehicle; and
- not performing required service and preventive maintenance.

The staff at Quality Equipment & Spray share these lessons to help others learn from them. We started writing articles for publications in the pest control, landscape and golf industries, as well as writing a blog at SprayEquipmentBlog.com.

This book is a consolidation of learning and articles from the past 10 years. By reviewing the concepts and techniques herein, you'll be able to:

- buy spray equipment right the first time;
- support your company brand;
- extend spray equipment life;
- reduce spray equipment downtime;
- reduce missed appointments;
- reduce spray equipment repair expense; and
- improve safety.

WHO THIS BOOK IS FOR
& HOW TO USE IT

This book is for:

- *Pest control company owners and managers;*
- *Weed control and landscape company owners and managers;*
- *Pest, weed and termite control technicians;*
- *Golf course equipment managers;*
- *Government and municipal spray equipment managers; and*
- *All serious users of spray equipment.*

If you haven't purchased your spray equipment, read the book cover to cover. If you already have spray equipment and are looking for easy pointers, read Part 5 - Spray Equipment Policies for Safety, Savings and Productivity and the quality tips found in the Appendix. If you're having a specific problem with hose reels, for example, read the chapter dedicated to that topic.

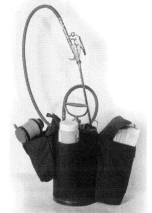

1

SPRAY EQUIPMENT STRATEGY: PLAN BEFORE YOU BUY

Many companies end up with the wrong spray equipment because they didn't take the time to plan their strategy and purchases. The old carpenter's adage, "measure twice, cut once" is relatable to spray equipment. It's important to understand company strategy drives spray equipment strategy, not vice versa. Selecting the wrong spray equipment will cause problems, from altering application protocol to significant decreases of technician productivity and scheduling.

A. Common spray equipment purchasing errors

It's amazing how much money companies spend buying the wrong power spray equipment. What are some of the causes of this problem, and what can be done to reduce purchasing mistakes and dollars wasted on spray equipment? Here are some common mistakes:

- **Buying one sprayer to meet all your spray needs.** When designing a sprayer to use for all possible needs and applications, the sprayer often does none of them well. For example, if a landscape company wants a sprayer to do pre- and post-weed control, deep root fertilization and tall-tree spraying, they'll probably end up with a rig that doesn't do a good job on any of them. Determine which applications will comprise 80 percent of the work for that vehicle, and design a sprayer to solve that problem. Find another way to solve the other 20 percent.

- **Buying the wrong equipment.** Here's an example: A pest control company bought a sprayer because it was available on the day the purchaser walked into the vendor's shop. When company employees started using the sprayer, they weren't getting the pressure or volume they needed. One quick look at the equipment explained why. The sprayer was built with a centrifugal pump and 300 feet of half inch hose. Centrifugal pumps are designed for volume, not pressure. This is a physics problem: The low-pressure centrifugal pump couldn't push the chemical through that much hose. Make sure components are matched properly. A second example is buying the wrong size tank. A tank that's too small reduces productivity because of the time needed to fill it up. A tank that's too big doesn't allow enough storage space on the truck, plus the water weight impacts gas mileage and truck repair expense.

- **Buying solely on price.** Too many companies look only at the purchase price of equipment, not the actual cost or value. An example of value: Some gas engines cost more than most other engines, but they'll last longer, start on the first pull and have fewer problems. Replacement part availability is another important factor.

    Another example of cost: The same spray tech who bought the aforementioned sprayer with the centrifugal pump, broke the pull cord on the gas engine. Because the recoil was too close to the side of the vehicle, the sprayer had to be unbolted and removed from the utility vehicle to replace the pull cord. A 10-minute job became an hour-long job. The company paid the spray tech to sit and wait, while paying more for repairs than would've been necessary had the sprayer been designed properly.

- **Viewing spray equipment as an expense, rather than a strategic investment.** Expenses are to be reduced, and investments are to be optimized. As a strategic investment, your sprayer will support your brand, marketing, operating and employee retention strategies.

  Example 1: A custom rig will cost more than one off the shelf. With a custom rig that allows an extra toolbox on a vehicle, a technician can carry equipment to offer additional services at the client location (e.g., rodent, bee, animal capture, exclusion, etc.).

  Example 2: An electric hose reel adds about $350 to the cost of a rig, but this investment is small if a technician can do one extra job a month or doesn't quit to work for another company that pays more, or the company avoids sick time for a tech's back injury.

- **Not getting enough input on the requirements.** Too many managers think they know everything about spray equipment and tell vendors what they want instead of asking for advice. Don't assume you know everything. Get advice about designing the equipment from employees and colleagues. When you attend an industry class or conference, walk through the parking lot, and look at competitor's equipment. Develop a relationship with your spray equipment vendor, and spend the time explaining your company's spray objectives. Another common problem is when a company buys a truck assuming the equipment will fit. Equipment doesn't always fit as desired, so ask for help early and often.

To design the best sprayer, get input from everyone involved. Here's a partial list of stakeholders and questions to ask:

- **Spray technicians**
  - ➤ What do you like and dislike about the equipment?
  - ➤ What would you change?
  - ➤ What would you like to see in the equipment?

- **Management**
  - ➤ Will the size or type of spray projects change?
  - ➤ Will the products (chemicals) change?
  - ➤ What vehicle(s) will the equipment go in?
  - ➤ Will one tech or multiple techs be using the equipment?

- **Maintenance department**
  - ➤ What do you like and dislike about the equipment?
  - ➤ What would you change?
  - ➤ Are there any components or design features that are problematic?

- **Purchasing department**
  - ➤ Will this work be multiple bid or directed to a specific vendor under contract?
  - ➤ Can we include the first year's maintenance parts as part of the purchase?
  - ➤ What would you like to see as part of the equipment?

- **Spray equipment vendor** (if not a multiple bid situation)
  - ➤ What recommendations do you have based on our application?
  - ➤ Here are some problems we have with our equipment.
  - ➤ How can you help us?

> ➢ Are spare parts readily available?
> ➢ What maintenance is likely to be required during the first year?
> ➢ Will this sprayer be easy for our users to operate?
> ➢ Will you train our users?

- **Bad or incomplete specifications.** When the department doesn't take the time to write clear, detailed specifications for the new sprayer, what you get might not be what you want or need. Here are examples:

> ➢ A municipality ordered a 300-gallon spray trailer with a 20-foot boom to control weeds in large fields. It stated that, aside from occasional weed spot spraying with the hose, this was the only application for this sprayer. A couple months later, they complained the sprayer wasn't working. When we went to see what was wrong, one tech was trying to spray 40-foot-tall trees, something the sprayer wasn't designed to do.

> ➢ Another government agency bid for three 200-gallon spray trailers and accepted the low bid. After three months, the pumps failed and were replaced numerous times before the agency called and asked us to take a look. The specification stated roller pump but didn't specify a model number. The vendor used the lowest grade pump, which couldn't tolerate herbicides. The same spray trailers used low-cost, low-quality plastic fittings in key places. A plastic fitting in the wrong place can fail, resulting in a chemical spill and lost productivity.

Be sure you know everything you're getting when ordering a sprayer. If you're going to bid, specify all components, not just the big ones. Sprayer specs must be detailed to ensure the desired outcome.

B. Company strategy should drive spray equipment selection

What spray equipment should a company buy? Why do technicians seem to take so long on each stop? How can the company boost productivity? These are some of the questions companies should ask when considering spray equipment purchases.

Too many companies buy the lowest price equipment or the one that was available at the time. When selecting spray equipment, operating strategy should determine equipment selection.

- **Here are examples of operating strategy:**
  - ➢ Will the vehicle be servicing residential or commercial accounts?
  - ➢ What's the treatment plan for these accounts – inside, outside or both?
  - ➢ Will the technician be power spraying each property or using a compressed air sprayer for most stops?
  - ➢ How many gallons of product will be applied at each stop?
  - ➢ How many stops will the technician make each day?
  - ➢ Are there any difficult-to-reach application areas?
  - ➢ Are technicians trained as universal techs (they perform every service the company offers), or are they specialized?

Once these and similar questions have been asked and answered, the spray equipment selection process can begin.

C. Strategic questions to consider when evaluating new spray equipment

Can the benefits of the new equipment be financially quantified?

- **Will sales increase from** add-on sales to customers, acquisition of new customers, or ability to raise prices?

- **Will expenses be reduced by** a decrease of product (i.e., chemical) or product delivery cost, a decrease of service time, an increase in technician productivity or reduced downtime?

Consider all implementation costs and issues. Some of these items are obvious; some aren't.

- **Equipment-related questions**
  - ➢ What's the warranty, and what does it cover?
  - ➢ Are replacement and repair parts readily available, and what's the cost?
  - ➢ How long will it take to receive repair parts (i.e., how long will the equipment be down?)
  - ➢ Can service be performed in-house, or must the unit be serviced internally.
  - ➢ What's the expected reliability given normal operating conditions of temperature extremes, vigorous use, a bouncing vehicle, etc.
  - ➢ Will there be installation costs?
  - ➢ Are there any on-going vendor support, subscription or maintenance fees?
  - ➢ What's the expected life of the equipment?

- **People-related questions**
  - ➢ Will one technician or all technicians be trained?
  - ➢ How much training is required?
  - ➢ Who will provide the training, and where will it be conducted?
  - ➢ Can technicians troubleshoot problems with the equipment?

- **Vehicle-related questions**

> ➤ Is there enough space on the vehicle to store or install the equipment?
> ➤ How will the equipment be packed and secured to prevent damage and theft?
> ➤ Will additional documentation – such as material safety data sheets (MSDS), Occupational Safety and Heath Administration (OSHA) information, etc. – be required on the truck?

If equipment costs are significant, consider asking the vendor for references of other companies using the equipment. Obviously, you'll only get the names of satisfied customers, but you might gain valuable insight about the product.

D. Spray equipment should support the company brand

Your brand is everything your company does in the marketplace to differentiate itself from competitors. Logos, advertising, operations plan, trucks, uniforms, etc., contribute to your brand. What comes to mind when you think about the following companies: Walmart, Apple computers and Starbucks? How many millions of dollars have these companies spent to create their brands, and how many billions are those brands worth? How would a customer feel if she walked into a Starbucks and the barista's uniform was filthy or the store had a foul odor? These companies work diligently to prevent negative impressions that conflict with their brand.

A pest control company also has a brand. A company can spend a lot of money on trucks, logos, signage, uniforms, business cards, forms, etc. A company can spend a lot of money on marketing and advertising to tell people how great it is. A company also can spend a lot of time and money developing an operating program and training technicians. In today's competitive market, branding is

What does this equipment say about this company? What will customers think of your company when they see this mess?

critical. Is the spray equipment a company uses supporting and contributing to its brand or detracting from it?

Examine these specifics:

- **Professional.** Does the spray equipment present a professional image? Is the equipment in good shape, or is it duct taped together? Is it of reasonable age, or is it ancient? Is the hose spliced in 17 places?

- **Neat / organized.** Is the equipment conveying the message the company is well organized? Can technicians access key components easily, or do they struggle to reach equipment? Must they dig through piles of stuff to get what they need, or is it readily available? Remember the business adage a cluttered desk means a cluttered mind? The same applies to company vehicles.

- **Signage.** Does the equipment maximize opportunities for signage?

- **Image.** Is the appearance of company trucks and equipment consistent with the company's brand?

- **Free of debris.** Is the truck free of debris? Does the tech use the bed as a trash can? Do chemicals build up in the bed or around the tank?

- **Clean.** Is the truck and equipment always spotless? A dirty truck sends a message to customers that the company doesn't care about cleanliness or safety. Customers might think that if the company doesn't care enough to keep its own property (truck and equipment) neat and clean, why would it care any more about the customer's property? If your equipment isn't clean, techs won't stay clean. Their uniforms will pick up chemical stains and odors from contact with the vehicle and equipment.

- **Easy to clean.** Has the equipment been designed for easy cleaning, or does it seem like it was designed to accumulate dirt? If the equipment has been designed for easy cleaning, it will be much easier to get your technicians to clean the vehicle regularly. If it's a hassle to clean, they won't do it.

Look at the equipment from the customer's perspective. Is the equipment sending the message the company wants and intends? Continually emphasize the technicians' and truck's appearance is important to the company's image in the marketplace. Work with the equipment provider to ensure equipment is designed to be neat, well-organized and easy to clean. Inspect vehicles to ensure they remain spotless. Provide positive recognition to employees who support the brand by keeping the equipment neat.

E. Protecting and retaining employees: Is your spray equipment up to the challenge?

Many companies state their employees are their greatest assets. These companies implement benefits and reward systems to attract and retain the best people. Many demographic changes are affecting the available labor pool. As a result, the workforce is aging, younger workers demand more from a job than just a paycheck, and younger workers have more employment options. Good employees are difficult to find, so companies need to do more to create a desirable work environment for the employees. Because of changes in the U.S. workforce, it's critical for companies to ask and answer the following question:

- **Does my spray equipment strategy support my human resource strategy?**

Here are considerations to help evaluate spray equipment to see if it's up to the challenge of protecting and retaining your employees, specifically spray technicians.

- **Is the equipment as safe as it can be?**

The first and most obvious consideration is safety. Have all the equipment hazards been minimized? Have you looked at your equipment closely to identify bump, scrape, abrasion, cut and burn hazards? Are all moving parts protected? Is the load secure, balanced and appropriate for the truck's capacity? Are chemicals building up in the truck, creating an exposure or slip hazard? Has the equipment been designed to eliminate unnecessary reaching and awkward actions that can

This company looks out for it's employees: electric reel makes the job easier, raising the reel reduces employee bending & stretching.

cause back strain? This last question is particularly crucial with an aging workforce. Remember, employees might have other employment options with fewer potential hazards.

- **Three ways to find the answer to these questions are:**
  - ➢ ask the employees;
  - ➢ spend a day riding with employees and observe the equipment in use in the field; and
  - ➢ management should occasionally use the equipment to identify hazards and annoyances.

- **Is the equipment reliable?** Most spray technicians want to do a good job servicing customers. They can't do that if equipment is unreliable and breaks down often. Employees with some component of variable compensation are particularly sensitive to equipment reliability problems. Unreliable equipment can be a leading cause of job dissatisfaction for spray technicians.

Has the spray equipment been designed for reliability? Are key components readily accessible for preventive maintenance? Can spray technicians access key components such as the line strainer (filter) to prevent problems from occurring? Are high-quality components used? When analyzing component quality, don't just consider expensive parts such as engines and pumps. Even low-cost items such as fittings and clamps can be reliability killers.

- **Does the equipment help boost productivity?** Is the equipment designed for productivity so spray technicians can meet company and personal objectives? Are extra steps required for simple activities because of the way the equipment is positioned? Are commonly accessed components strategically placed for productivity?

   Again, observe how employees use the equipment in the field. Ask them for ideas about improving equipment productivity. Some equipment upgrades might be justified through productivity gains. Some companies use electric-rewind hose reels, not just as a productivity improvement, but as a way to retain employees. Rolling up 300 feet of water-laden chemical hose in the afternoon sun can be tiring and unpleasant. One additional residential service per month will more than pay for the incremental cost of the electric reel. Look for equipment productivity efficiencies to improve operating results and employee satisfaction.

- **Summary.** Scrutinize your company's spray equipment to determine if it's helping attract and retain employees. Involve employees and vendors in this review. Employees will appreciate the interest in their safety and well-being and will likely be excited about contributing to the success of the company. Safety issues should be addressed immediately. Other improvements can be built into future equipment designs when equipment is replaced. Conduct this review regularly until you've designed the optimal pest management equipment for your company and employees.

F. Purchase price is the tip of the iceberg

Many companies never calculate what pest control or weed control spray equipment costs their company.

Many managers equate spray equipment cost with the purchase price. Unfortunately, purchase price is only one component of cost. It's only the tip of the iceberg. The majority of spray equipment cost is like the bulk of the iceberg – unseen, waiting to sink your company.

- **Total equipment cost includes the following:** purchase price, installation, maintenance and repairs, productivity, and longevity/replacement.

- **Purchase price is the most obvious component of total cost.** Unfortunately, it's often the only cost considered in a purchase decision. Purchase price includes total purchase price of the base unit plus any optional equipment, sales tax and freight.

- **Installation cost includes the total cost of installing the equipment in the vehicle.** Generally, rigs requiring electric power will cost more to install. This equipment must be wired to the truck battery, which takes more time and requires wire, fuse, etc. Ask your rig vendor if electrical components are included in the purchase price. More complex sprayers, such as those with booms or electric

How equipment affects daily productivity is a significant expense impact. To put gas in this engine, all the hose must be unrolled off the reel.

or digital controls, will be more costly to install.

If installing the rig in house, be sure to know what's under the truck bed. Drilling through the bed into the gas tank adds significant cost. Note: This observation is based on personal experience.

- **Maintenance cost is planned and includes engine oil changes, pump rebuilds, spray gun rebuilds, etc.** Maintenance costs include the cost of the components and labor. Regular maintenance will extend the life of a sprayer. Repairs are unplanned and involve repairing or replacing problem components. Consider these maintenance and repair factors:
  - ➢ Are replacement parts available?
  - ➢ Is there clear access to equipment to perform the service?

> ➤ Will the maintenance be done in-house or by a vendor?
> ➤ Is the maintenance easy to do, or are special skills or tools required?

Remember the aforementioned example involving the sprayer in the ATV with a broken engine pull cord. Because of the rig design, the pull cord couldn't be replaced without first removing the skid from the ATV first. A 10-minute task became a one-hour job. Think about what this does to maintenance costs if you must remove the rig to do something easy like change the oil. Make sure equipment is designed to allow for easy maintenance. If a sprayer isn't designed for maintenance, then maintenance will be delayed or ignored, and equipment problems will occur.

- **Repair costs.** Does the rig constantly break down? Repair cost includes not just the cost of the repair but the downtime that results and any appointments missed or cancelled. Are replacement parts readily available? Waiting for parts to be shipped in from the manufacturer can be a productivity killer.

- **Productivity impact.** Does the equipment boost technician productivity or hinder it? Are key components properly situated for easy, safe, ergonomic access? Must a technician perform extra (wasted) motions just to do the job?

This is the most important cost of a power sprayer because it affects the technician on every stop, every day. Wage expenses are the largest expense of most pest and weed control companies. For pest control companies with revenues of $150,000 to $25 million a year, wage expense ranges from 42 to 48 percent of sales. (Source: NPMA 2010 Business

Development Operating Ratio Survey, page 19). Anything the company can do to make a technician more efficient and effective has a direct bottom line impact. Hiring good techs, training them well, designing tight concentrated routes, having reliable spray equipment that supports or boosts technicians' productivity are money makers.

- **Longevity / replacement cost.** How long do the components last? Are high-quality components used?

The following are examples:

- One of the most expensive components of a sprayer is the gas engine. Some cost more than others, but the more expensive ones will provide years of uninterrupted service if they're maintained properly. This isn't an area in which to save a few dollars. The higher upfront cost is more than offset in reduced repairs and downtime and extended life.

- Some of the cheapest components of a power sprayer are the plumbing fittings, yet these inexpensive parts can cost a bundle. A plastic fitting in the wrong place can be damaged easily, resulting in chemical spillage and lost productivity. Understand everything you're getting when ordering a sprayer.

- Here's a final example from a large pest control company. The local office orders rigs from its national office, which buys in bulk to save money. The rigs are delivered to the local equipment shop, where techs make improvements and modifications requested by local management before installing the rig. The rig purchase is booked by national as a capital expenditure, and the extensive modifications are booked locally as repairs. The company doesn't know the total cost of the equipment.

- Don't assume purchase price is the same as cost. As professional owners and managers, it's critical to business success to understand total equipment costs. Learn where the icebergs lie.

G. Spray equipment selection: Start here

One of the first and most critical decisions when purchasing spray equipment is selecting a vendor. It's important to work with a company you trust. Select a vendor that has been around for awhile and has all the equipment your company needs. Too many companies spread their purchases around shopping for the lowest price. It's better to focus purchases with one company that will be there for you when you have a problem. When spray equipment breaks down, the few dollars saved by shopping around for the lowest price up front will seem insignificant. Here are criteria to use when selecting a vendor:

- **Reliability.** Has it been around, and will it be around?

- **Expertise.** Is it an expert in the field? Does it have expertise with the equipment it sells, or is it just an 800 number with a $10-an-hour telephone rep on the other end?

- **Inventory.** Remember, spray equipment wears out. Sure it has sold you the widget for $10 less, but does it have the replacement parts, repair kits, etc., needed to service the equipment once it has been used vigorously for a year?

- **Good fit.** Companies consist of people. Does the vendor fit with your company? Does it listen to your concerns? Does it make recommendations? Does it want to help? If you're not comfortable dealing with it, find another.

- **Does the vendor sell you what it has on the shelf**, or does it listen to understand what you need and provide that?

Additional principles to consider when buying spray equipment:

- **Quality.** Buy quality stuff, and take care of it. It's much cheaper in the long run.

- **Replacement parts.** Always buy equipment for which replacement parts, repair kits, etc., are readily available. There's nothing worse than having a piece of equipment break down and a technician waiting for a $5 part.

- **Standardize the equipment.** This is one of the most important things a company can do to create a rational spray equipment program.

Here are additional considerations when selecting and designing your spray equipment:

- **Ease of use.** The sprayer must be easy for spray technicians to use. Key components must be easily accessible so the tech can reach them easily. The sprayer must be easy to operate. If controls are too complex, there will be problems that cost the company money. Example: a large state agency purchased a computerized right-of-way sprayer to spray weeds along the highway. The controls were so complicated, the agency couldn't find techs who could operate the equipment.

- **Ease of maintenance.** All sprayers require maintenance. Many companies and techs don't maintain equipment regularly. If maintenance is difficult, the odds of it occurring decline significantly.

  If components are difficult to service, maintenance will take much longer, which means more downtime and higher costs. Example: A power spray rig was designed so the spray rig had to be removed from the vehicle and the hose reel unbolted from the rig to change the hose reel swivels. This is standard annual maintenance that should take 10 minutes or less. On this sprayer, it took two hours.

- **Think about these questions:**
  - ➢ What maintenance will be required on this equipment?
  - ➢ How easy will it be to perform maintenance?
  - ➢ Is it easy to change the engine oil?
  - ➢ Is it easy to remove the pump for service?
  - ➢ Can the water flow from the tank be shut off so downstream components can be removed for service without spilling chemicals?
  - ➢ Is it easy to access the hose reel swivel for maintenance?
  - ➢ What other maintenance will be required, and how easy will it be to do?

It's much easier, faster and cheaper to think about these questions before the sprayer requires maintenance.

H. Equipment standardization: It works for Southwest Airlines; it will work for you

Have you noticed Southwest Airlines makes money year after year? It makes money regardless of the economy. It

Standardization is one of the best equipment decisions you'll make.

makes money even when its competitors lose money. So how does Southwest Airlines do it? There are a number of reasons for their success, including great management and culture, and the use of a point-to-point system of flight scheduling (rather than the more complex hub-and-spoke system used by most major airlines). Another reason it always excels is standardized equipment. The airline flies only one type of aircraft – the Boeing 737, which creates considerable efficiencies. For example:

- **Training.** All staff needs to be trained on only one aircraft. This applies to pilots, cabin staff, ground staff, baggage handlers, mechanics, accountants, marketing managers, telephone service and maintenance staff.

- **Scheduling.** All staff can work on any aircraft. For example, if a pilot is sick, any other pilot do the job without additional training or instruction. This reduces the odds of having to cancel a flight when the appropriate staff isn't available. Additionally, any Southwest plane can taxi up to any airport, terminal or gate to which Southwest flies.

- **Efficiency.** Every employee knows exactly where everything is and how to do their job, no matter which plane or flight they're working, supporting or servicing.

- **Maintenance.** Mechanics only need to be trained to service one plane. The capital (cash) tied up in parts inventories and tools is much lower because there are so many fewer required parts. This also significantly improves the odds a needed part will be available to solve a problem, which, in turn, reduces the downtime the planes are on the ground not producing revenue. In the extreme, the number of backup aircraft Southwest must keep available is lower than its competitors that fly multiple types of aircraft.

These concepts also apply to companies using spray equipment. Standardizing spray equipment will result in many of the same efficiencies for the company.

Here are ideas to get started.

- **If your equipment is standardized, congratulations.** You're in the minority. Take the next step and standardize storage locations for the vehicles. For example, marker flags are always stored in location X. Even companies with large fleets and standardized equipment have significant variations among trucks because techs keep their tools and materials in different places.

- **It doesn't make sense to replace all equipment with new, standardized equipment**, so start small with key components that can have a big impact.

Suggestions:

- **Line strainer / filter.** Filters are the source of many problems. Start here. Standardize filters so all techs know how to check and change them and it's easy and cheap to inventory the screens and gaskets that cause so many problems.

- **Quick disconnects.** Standardize quick disconnects and spray tools on all trucks so spray guns are interchangeable and a leaking gun doesn't disrupt schedules.

- **Develop equipment standards.** Create clear standards for hand sprayers, backpack sprayers, tool boxes, power sprayers, etc., As obsolete equipment is replaced, the fleet becomes standardized.

- **Common sense required.** You might not be able to standardize everything. On special purpose vehicles, standardize where you can. For example, on a larger vehicle for commercial work, while most of the fleet does residential work, you still can work with your equipment vendor to standardize filtration (location, access, design) and maintenance (engine positioned so oil changes are easy).

Start now by examining equipment to find opportunities. Even a little standardization can go a long way toward improved service, productivity and profitability.

I. Spray equipment and integrated pest management (IPM)

The purpose of this book isn't to explain or advocate for IPM; however, it's important to discuss how IPM affects equipment. IPM doesn't mean doing the same with a natural product in your spray tank. Converting to a green pest control program requires a reevaluation of the spray equipment strategy to make sure it supports your IPM strategy.

IPM relies heavily on the principles of inspection, identification, monitoring and custom answers. Look at your equipment to make sure the tools are available to give your customers the service the company has committed to providing.

- **Design and layout.** IPM requires more tools than traditional pest control. Is the equipment in the truck efficiently designed and organized so you can carry all the tools you need?

- **Storage.** IPM requires additional storage (locking toolboxes, tool lockers, etc.) to keep materials separate

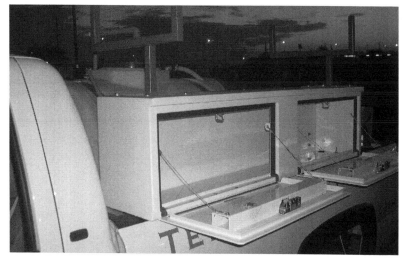

IPM might require the use of more products that need to be stored separately to prevent contamination. An addititional toolbox might be a good idea.

and uncontaminated. Is there sufficient storage for needed tools and equipment? For example, an IPM program likely will use much larger quantities of glue boards and insect monitors, which must be kept clean and free from odor, so they should be stored separately from pesticides.

- **Cleanliness.** Customers looking for green pest control are more likely to insist on professionalism and cleanliness, which starts with the truck, equipment and technicians. Is the equipment designed so it can be cleaned easily, or does it build up debris and chemicals that contaminate equipment and technician uniforms? There are numerous design changes a good equipment provider can make to ensure equipment can be cleaned easily.

IPM might require additional tools or products. A multi-function IPM Toolbelt might come in handy.

- **Safety.** IPM might require multiple tools where one sufficed previously. For example, most traditional pest management professionals (PMPs) use one compressed air sprayer. Custom solutions might require multiple sprayers for multiple products. Is the equipment secured in the vehicle so it doesn't loosen and leak, damage equipment or become airborne if a crash happens?

- **Multiple tanks.** Custom IPM solutions might require multiple spray tanks for multiple products to prevent contamination. Some PMPs have used multiple tanks and one pump and hose. This type of contamination might not be acceptable with green products. Work with the equipment provider to design the best equipment solution for the IPM operations plan.

- **Custom solutions.** Some customers transitioning to green pest control have required custom equipment solutions to support their programs. A little time invested in a conversation about your green program and operational needs might result in a new design that will save your technicians time or allow them to do a more effective job servicing your customers. Examples include custom storage, custom foamers, multiple tank units and specialized spray units.

- **Maintenance.** Be aware of the impact of different

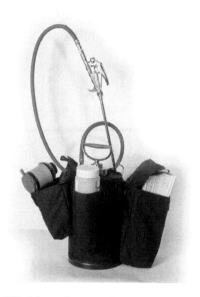

IPM might require additional tools or products. You might need to be creative about storing these products on the vehicle.

IPM might require new tools and rethinking your equipment strategy.

products on your equipment. For example, some natural botanical-based pesticides are much harsher on rubber than traditional pesticides, which could cause o-rings and gaskets to wear out faster. Some borate products might require additional cleaning to prevent chemical build up, which might require you to update your preventive maintenance programs or store additional parts on the vehicle for quick in-the-field repairs by technicians.

IPM programs require you to reevaluate your pest and weed management equipment. Taking time to ensure your equipment supports the IPM program will save you time and improve the green service you provide to customers.

Select the tank size based on size, number of daily jobs and vehicle capacity.

POWER SPRAY COMPONENTS

A. Start with the tank

- **Tank size is critical.** The first component of a power spray rig is the tank. Once tank size is determined, every other component can be selected. Tank size should be the largest one needed to support the average or expected daily workload. Select a tank large enough so a technician isn't constantly refilling, which kills productivity and can annoy customers who don't like vendors using the customer's water. The tank must be small enough to fit in the truck and keep the load (weight of the water) within the truck's safe handling

    If the company hasn't yet acquired the vehicle, use this formula to determine tank size:

Average number of stops per day
X
Average number of gallons applied per stop
+
small safety margin

= recommended tank size

Example: The plan is to make 12 stops per day and apply 5 gallons of product per stop.

$$12 \text{ stops} \times 5 \text{ gallons} = 60 \text{ gallons}$$
$$+$$
$$5\% \text{ safety factor } (3 \text{ gallons}) = \textbf{63 gallons}$$

Tanks don't come in 63-gallon sizes, but the next larger size is 65 gallons, which is the minimum starting point (in this example).

It's better to have too many gallons than not enough. Having to stop to refill the tank will hurt productivity and often angers the customer whose water you're using to fill the tank. Remember, a larger tank can always be partially filled if that's all the day's workload requires.

If a tank is 100 gallons, but the tech knows he'll only need 50 gallons for the day's work, fill the tank halfway, which is preferable to having a 50-gallon tank and having to refill it to finish the day's jobs. This assumes the truck has the capacity (weight and space) to handle the tank.

If a company already has a vehicle, tank size might be limited. For example, don't put more than 50 or 65 gallons in a compact pickup truck. Those who put too large a tank in a small truck pay for it by having to frequently replace brakes, tires, suspension and transmission.

Most power sprayer tanks are made from polyethylene, a form of plastic, fiberglass or metal (usually steel or aluminum). Pros and cons of each include:

- **Poly tanks**
  Pros:
  - ➢ It's the least expensive type of tank.
  - ➢ It's usually easy to see water level inside the tank.
  - ➢ They're relatively cheap and easy to replace.
  - ➢ They can be plumbed from the top or bottom.

➤ They're usually manufactured by large companies and are available nationally.

Cons:
➤ It might not last as long as other types of tanks.

- **Fiberglass tanks**
Pros:
  ➤ They're durable.
  ➤ You can put advertising on the tank (e.g., phone number, company logo, etc.).

  Cons:
  ➤ They're more expensive than poly.
  ➤ They usually can only be plumbed from the top.
  ➤ You can't tell how much water is in tank unless a sight gauge is installed.
  ➤ They often require a steel frame for support, which adds cost and weight.
  ➤ They're more difficult to replace. Because fiberglass tanks are made locally with a custom mold, they can only be replaced by the company that built them. If that company has changed tank design or is no longer in business, the tank won't be available, and it's likely significant sprayer modifications will be required to install a replacement tank.

- **Metal tanks**
Pros:
  ➤ They're the most durable.
  ➤ They can be plumbed from the top or bottom. You can put advertising on the tank (e.g., phone number, company logo, etc.).

  Cons:
  ➤ They're the most expensive.

➤ They can add considerable weight to the sprayer.

➤ You can't tell how much water is in the tank unless a sight gauge is installed.

➤ They can get hot under the summer sun

B. Spray hose: Too much isn't enough

Considerations for power sprayer hose selection are:

- **Diameter.** Most common weed and pest spray applications include 3/8 inch or ½ inch inside diameter (ID) spray hoses on power spray rigs. A larger diameter hose delivers more volume. A larger hose costs more and is heavier to pull out and wind up. The weight can be a factor for the technician at the end of a long day. Some applications, such as pretreating termite or spraying tall trees, might require larger ID hose. Conversely, a smaller ID hose delivers less volume but weighs less and costs less than larger ID hose. A smaller diameter hose results in more pressure loss because of increased friction of the water moving through the hose. If the application requires significant pressure, consider a larger ID hose. Examples of applications requiring higher pressure are spraying tall trees or throwing water horizontally over a large distance – a nursery with large rows of trees, for example. (For a useful chart about calculating pressure loss, download a spraying guide at www.qspray.com/sprayingguide).

- **Length.** It's risky to use words such as always or never because they often get you in trouble. When it comes to spray hose, it's always better to have too much hose rather than not enough. If the hose is one foot too short, you can't complete the job. Longer hose enables you to spray difficult-to-reach places. With a longer hose, when the hose end wears out, it can be cut off without having to purchase new hose. The additional upfront cost of the extra hose is well worth the investment. If a longer hose is only used on rare occasions, put the extra hose on quick disconnects and attach it when needed. Spray hose usually comes in 200 - and 300 - foot rolls. Most suppliers will charge for the full roll, so there's usually no benefit buying a partial roll.

- **Pressure.** Be sure the hose has a burst pressure that significantly exceeds the maximum pressure rating of the spray pump you're using. You don't want the hose to burst and spill chemical while spraying.

- **Cost and quality.** Hose prices have increased recently because spray hose is made from petroleum products and transportation is a significant component of the cost. There are huge variations of hose quality and cost, so generalizations are difficult to make. Some hose remains flexible in cold weather, and some hose lasts longer despite being pulled across rocks or around corners of buildings. When you find a hose you like, stick with it. Less expensive hose that doesn't last will cost more in the long run.

Problems

- **Wear.** When the hose is showing significant wear – cuts, scrapes, gouges, etc. – fix it. Don't wait for it to leak. It will cost much more in lost productivity to stop in the middle of a job, drive to the repair shop and return to the jobsite. The first 30 feet is where hose will break down first. When significant wear occurs, cut out the bad portion. This is another reason to start with a longer spray hose.

- **Temperature.** Significant temperature extremes can reduce hose life. Whenever possible, protect hose from extreme heat and cold.

- **Pressure problems.** Occasionally, spray hose can degrade pest sprayer performance. If everything appears to be working properly but you're not getting any pressure, it could be a hose problem. If your hose is wound too tightly on the reel, the hose could flatten out and provide sufficient resistance so you don't get the output you require. This condition might occur on some low-pressure, 12-volt electric pumps. To correct this problem, unwind the hose, turn on the pump and rewind the hose onto the reel less tightly. Another problematic situation occurs when old hose becomes spongy. The hose expands, significantly reducing the pressure that can be achieved at the hose end. Replace the hose.

Don't wait for hose to fail. Cut off bad hose before a chemical spill or downtime occurs.

- **Policies and procedures.** Technicians should run the hose through a rag while rewinding the hose onto the reel. This removes debris that can cut or damage hose.

  Train technicians to inspect spray hoses, especially the first 30 feet or so, where problems are most likely to occur. A quick inspection for puddles under the reel will identify leaks on inner portions of hose. Encourage technicians to report problems and leaks, rather than living with them.

  The inside section of the hose (closest to the reel) experiences the least wear. Periodically reverse the hose to extend overall life.

  Provide technicians with hose repair kits so temporary repairs can be performed in the field, which allows technicians to finish their route before bringing the truck in for a more permanent hose repair. A repair kit consisting of hose mender, clamps, knife and screw driver can be inexpensively assembled.

  Supervisors should perform regular truck inspections and check hose for wear and leaks.

  Buying the right hose, then preventing hose problems is a lot cheaper than cleaning up chemical spills and causing downtime. A proactive approach to your hose will save time and money.

C.   Hose reels

- **Selection.** Buy a quality, name-brand reel. Be sure replacement parts are readily available. It's much easier to buy replacement parts on standard color reels. An electric rewind reel will increase cost because of purchase price, electrical components and additional installation requirements. Many companies believe the additional cost is more than offset by increased technician productivity.

Roller guides keep the hose in front of the reel, which keeps the hose off the vehicle, extending hose life and protecting the vehicle. By keeping the hose in front of the reel, roller guides make it easier to pull hose when a technician is away from the vehicle.

- **Installation.** Install the reel so it's easy for technician to reach and operate without any unnatural reaching or stretching. If most stops are residential and the vehicle will be parked at the curb, side mounting the reel makes sense. For passenger side mount reels, this often means raising the reel off the truck bed. Consider driver visibility when installing the reel.

  If the reel is to face the rear of the truck, mounting the reel at bed level might be more visually appealing. The downside is the tailgate must be dropped at each stop to access the reel.

  For electric reels, use only a push button (or momentary) switch so the reel can't be left in the on position, which will damage reel, hose or gun. Be sure the push button is conveniently located for technician access. Install a solenoid and fuse to protect the reel motor. Make sure there's no reel lock on electric reels, because if the reel is locked when the tech pushes the button, damage will occur.

  We don't recommend hanging any plumbing on the reel swivel because the extra weight puts torque on swivel O-rings, reducing life and causing leaks. Make sure there's play in the feeder hose to allow the swivel to rotate freely.

- **Maintenance.** The hose reel swivel is the area requiring the most attention. It will leak eventually. We recommend replacing the O-rings annually before your busy season. Don't wait for the O-rings to leak and disrupt your schedule. If you have standardized reels on your vehicles, it makes sense to keep O-ring kits in inventory.

A common problem is when the swivel usually starts to leak with a slow drip. Technicians often ignore this drip, thinking it's not a big deal. The slow drip quickly becomes a steady stream that can't be ignored. Don't wait for problems like this.

Periodically inspect the reel lock. A broken or missing reel lock can allow the hose to unroll, which is a time waster and potential safety hazard.

- **Repairs.** Other than swivels, reels usually are reasonably trouble-free. Eventually, the center hub might rust out and require replacement. Your equipment provider probably stocks this part.

Hanging lots of heavy plumbing on the hose reel swivel will reduce O-ring life and causes leaks.

Installing the hub is a big job and requires removing all the spray hose and dismantling the reel.

On electric reels, the solenoid, push button and fuse will require replacement eventually. Reel motors are usually durable, but if they fail, they can be rewired by a local motor shop. Some electric reels are chain driven, so periodically inspect the chain for excessive wear or stretching.

Rubber orings in hose reel swivel will leak eventually. Keep a repair kit on hand and change O-rings before the leak worsens.

D. Power sprayer motor

The first question to consider is whether to buy a gas or electric motor sprayer. Here are pros and cons of each:

Pros of an electric motor

- **Lower cost.** Electric sprayers generally are simpler, have fewer parts and cost significantly less than gas-powered ones. Usually, the pump and motor are a single unit, which costs less than gas powered ones and doesn't require additional assembly, which saves labor and cost.

- **Less space.** Electric sprayers generally take up less space in a vehicle. The electric pump and motor usually is significantly smaller than a gas motor and pump assembly. The smaller footprint has a number of advantages:

  ➢ Ability to use a smaller vehicle. Smaller vehicles generally cost less to purchase and operate.
  More space for other equipment and products.

- **Less maintenance.** Electric power sprayers have fewer moving parts and often have simpler plumbing. This means less can go wrong, fewer parts to maintain in inventory and easier maintenance.

- **Greener image.** Because they don't use gasoline, the operator can claim to be a greener company that doesn't use gas-burning engines. There's no need to store gas and oil.

- **Quieter.** Electric motors make almost no noise

compared to gas-powered sprayers, which can be noisy. This can allow the operator to work earlierc and later in the day without disturbing customers and neighbors.

Cons of an electric motor

- **Lower output.** Electric sprayers generally are lower output or volume (as measured in gallons per minute or GPM) than gas-powered sprayers. This means electric pumps generally aren't suited for high-volume jobs such as termite pretreats, large weed preemergent jobs or driving a large spray boom (e.g., golf course fairway sprayer).

- **Lower pressure.** Electric sprayers generally provide lower pressure than gas-powered sprayers. Pressure is measured in pounds per square inch or PSI. Electric pumps aren't suited for high-pressure jobs such as spraying tall trees

Electric motors are cheap, quiet and compact. They generally provide lower output (volume, pressure) than gas power.

or long distances. Longer hoses can be a problem for the lower-pressure electric pumps to push water through. Occasionally, spray hose problems can occur with low-pressure electric pumps. Two examples:

➢ The spray hose is old and mushy. It swells to absorb pressure, and there's no pressure left to push the water through the hose.

➢ The spray hose is wound too tightly on the reel, and the pump doesn't have enough pressure to push the water through the squished down hose.

• **Volume pressure tradeoff.** In addition to having less volume and pressure than gas-powered pumps, electric pumps usually have a significant tradeoff between volume and pressure. You can find a higher pressure electric pump, but it will be lower volume (and vice versa). On the other hand, gas-powered pumps are available in high volume, high pressure if needed – diaphragm pumps, for example.

• **Transferring sprayer to another vehicle.** Electric pumps usually are wired to the truck battery, so it's more involved to transfer the spray rig to another vehicle – the vehicle requires service, for example. The rig must be wired to the battery of the new vehicle. Contrast this to a gas-powered sprayer in which the power source is part of the sprayer. It just needs to be transferred to the backup vehicle. No wiring is required.

• **Fail points.** Experience shows that all 12-volt electric pumps commonly used for pest- and weed- control applications have weak points that fail. This book doesn't address or recommend vendors or models, but generally speaking:

> ➢ Smaller pumps are more reliable and draw fewer amps, which means they won't kill the truck battery. The downside to these pumps is the pressure demand switch is usually a weak point that fails about once a year. The pressure switch senses demand (i.e., you're squeezing the spray gun trigger) and turns the pump on. The constant off and on takes its toll on this switch, which is usually the first component to fail. This isn't a reason not to purchase an electric sprayer, it's merely maintenance to be planned.

The higher-volume pumps draw more amps and require one of the following:

> ➢ A separate battery in the vehicle to drive the pump; Running the vehicle while spraying so the battery doesn't die; or spraying for shorter periods, then starting the vehicle so the battery doesn't die.

Pros of a gas motor

- **Volume.** Gas sprayers generally can generate significantly more volume than electric-powered sprayers. This is helpful for applications where you need to apply a lot of product and you don't want it to take all day. Examples:

  > ➢ termite pretreats;
  > ➢ weed preemergent jobs;
  > ➢ driving a large spray boom or boomless nozzles;
  > ➢ large tanks requiring jet agitation; and
  > ➢ granular products requiring a lot of agitation to stay in suspension.

- **Pressure.** Gas-powered sprayers can generate more pressure than electric ones. Pressure is helpful when throwing water long distances. High pressure also can be useful when pushing water through a long hose and in varying droplet sizes. Example are spraying eves on homes, tall trees and distant, difficult-to-reach areas.

- **Selection.** There's a larger selection and variety of gas-powered pumps available for a pest or weed spray rig. It's easier to find the needed combination of volume and pressure with a gas-powered sprayer than it is with a 12-volt electric sprayer.

- **Vehicle flexibility.** Because the gas-powered sprayer has its own power source, it can be moved to another vehicle easier than an electric sprayer that relies on the vehicle's battery. This flexibility can come in handy if a vehicle is down or is needed for another purpose.

Cons of a gas motor

- **Higher cost.** Gas sprayer generally cost more than electric sprayers.

- **More space.** Gas sprayers generally take up more space in the vehicle.

- **More maintenance.** Gas motors have more moving parts and more complex plumbing than electric power sprayers. Gasoline must be carried on the vehicle to run the engine. The engine oil must be checked and refilled for proper operation.

- **No green image.** Because they use gasoline, these motors aren't considered green. Gas and oil must be stocked.

- **Noisy.** Gas engines can be quite noisy. During early or late hours, these engines might disturb customers and neighbors.

E. Power sprayer pump: the heart of the system

The pump is one of the most critical and costly components of a power spray rig. It's usually the component that requires the most service and experiences the most problems, so selection is critical. Pump selection should be based on:

- **Required output volume** (gallons per minute, GPM). GPM must be sufficient for the spray technician to do the job in a reasonable amount of time. Output also must be sufficient to provide jet agitation, if required.

Gas motors usually provide more power and volume, but they cost more and require more maintenance.

It's important to note the GPM specs provided by manufacturers are under ideal conditions, i.e., brand new pump, no line restrictions, no hose, etc. Pumps will supply less GPM than the manufacturer specs, even on day one. With a little wear, output might be significantly less than the specification.

- **Required pressure** (pounds per square inch, PSI). PSI must be sufficient for the pump to push the water through the hose then allow the technician to do the job. The longer the hose and the smaller the inside diameter of the hose, the more pressure is lost by the time the water reaches the spray gun. If the job requires throwing water over significant distances or heights, more pressure is required. Pumps will supply lower PSI than the manufacturer specs.

- **Material to be applied.** The material to be applied has a significant impact on pump selection. Some materials are tougher on pumps than others. Granular fertilizers are at the more difficult end of the scale; liquid pesticides are on the easier end. Select a pump that can withstand the material being applied, or the material will destroy the pump.

- **Cost versus performance.** There's a large variation in the cost of pumps. A more expensive pump might be worth the investment if it will get the job done faster or last longer than a less expensive one.

Other considerations

- **Are replacement parts readily available?**

- **Who will be doing the maintenance?** If it's the company,

select a pump that can be maintained easily by an
in-house mechanic.

- **Hard use.** Some companies and technicians are hard
  on pumps. If that's the case, select a pump that can
  withstand hard use.

- **Proper plumbing.** Ensure your equipment is plumbed
  properly according to manufacturer specifications.
  Examples of proper plumbing include:

  ➢ A proper input line size to feed the pump.
  ➢ A clear feed to pump (too many constrictions
    or turns on the input can place undue stress
    on pump).
  ➢ A line strainer/filter in front of pump to prevent
    debris from entering the pump.
  ➢ A shut-off valve on the input line to the pump so
    the pump can be removed easily for service even
    when the tank is full of water.
  ➢ Proper return (pressure relief) to tank. The return
    line should go to the top of the tank and shouldn't
    have any restrictions or shut-off valves on it. The

Perform preventive maintenance on pumps and
equipment before failure. This diaphragm pump is
a total loss because of the lack of PM.

Preventive maintenance, warning signs and
common sense were ignored, resulting in the
destruction of this roller pump.

return to the bottom of the tank makes it difficult to service the pump when the tank is full and the back pressure created by the weight of the water in the tank affects the pump. (Many pump manufacturers won't warranty a pump if the return is plumbed to the bottom of the tank.)

➤ Centrifugal pumps require a vent line return to prevent pump damage.

Connecting the pump to the motor

Most electric pumps come attached to the motor so this isn't a problem for electric power sprayers.

On gas-powered sprayers, the drive mechanism needs to be considered. There are three common ways to connect the pump to the engine:

- **Direct coupled.** The pump mounts directly to the engine. This is common on diaphragm pumps and the preferred mounting method because there are no exposed moving parts and no belts or rubber spiders to fail.

- **Jaw-style coupling.** Jaw-style couplings are placed on the pump and motor, and a rubber insert (spider) is placed in the middle of the two jaws. Many users prefer this method more than belts and pulleys because it occupies less space and they believe belts will fail. It's important to inspect the spider frequently and replace it when it's worn, or pump damage might occur. It's critical to place a protective guard over the spinning shafts (of the motor and pump) and the couplings. The downside to jaw-style couplings is they require a gear-reduced engine. These engines cost more than a regular engine and spin at a slower speed, so output is lower. This usually isn't a factor on new pumps, but lower output can be a factor when the pump is worn.

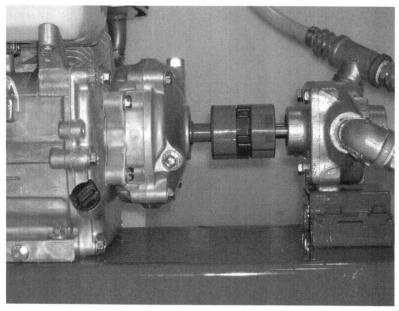

Jaw style coupling can save space, but pumps turn slower as a result so output is reduced.

- **Belts and pulleys.** Pulleys are placed on the pump and motor, and an automotive-style belt is used to drive the pump. It's critical to place a protective guard over the spinning shafts (of the motor and pump) and the pulleys. The downside to belts and pulleys is it takes more space, and when the belt gets worn, the pump won't turn. On the other hand, a worn belt won't harm the pump. Compare this to a worn jaw coupling spider, which can severely damage the pump if not replaced promptly.

Pump maintenance

Pump performance is critical to a technician's ability to perform his job. It's important to pay particular attention to the pump to identify problems and prevent damage.

Key points are:

- **Perform preventive maintenance.** Most pumps need to be rebuilt just about every year. Don't wait for the pump to fail during the busy season. Do the maintenance during slow time before or after the busy season.

- **Most pumps have some indicator of problems.** For example, roller pumps have weep holes that drip, diaphragm pumps have an oil reservoir that changes color, and gear pumps will drip from the packing nut when service is required. Train technicians to look and listen to pumps and report problems promptly. If you catch a problem early, it's usually faster and cheaper than ignoring the problem and waiting for the pump to fail.

- **Check the filter.** Train technicians to check the filter regularly. A clean filter prevents many pump problems.

- **Don't run it full out.** It's usually not necessary to run a pump at full speed. Continually running a pump in the red will reduce pump life.

F. Spray guns and tools

The choice of spray gun (or other spray tools) is mainly based on the application and personal preference. Factors to consider:

- **Choose quality equipment.** Most quality spray tools are made from brass, aluminum or steel. Most plastic guns are cheap. Buy a national name-brand gun.

- **Ask your equipment supplier which parts are likely to fail on the gun.** How is the gun rebuilt or repaired? If it's too difficult to rebuild, consider the gun a throwaway. It still might be worth purchasing, but consider the cost and longevity of the tool.

- **Standardize.** Whatever gun you select, standardize.

- **Are spare parts available?** If not, it's a throwaway. Keep an extra gun on hand as a backup, and keep spare parts and repair kits in inventory to make repairs.

- **Are multiple spray tips available for the gun?** You might not need a different tip today, but it's likely you'll need one in the future. The availability of multiple tips means you won't need to purchase another gun for that future job.

G. Spray tips

Pest- and weed-control power sprayers rely on spray tips for proper application of chemicals. The correct, well-maintained spray tip in a spray gun can contribute to excellent results – control of pests, weeds and expenses. The wrong or worn tip will have the opposite results.

Selection

The spray tip is the main determinate of power sprayer output. For example, it doesn't matter if you have a 20-gpm pump and 1-inch spray hose when the tip is just 1 GPM. Tip selection determines output volume and pattern and droplet size. Each of these factors impacts the quality of the application and the control you achieve.

Select quality spray tools, with ready availability of multiple tips and repair parts. Avoid plastic when possible.

Brass spray tips wear out at about 10% per year. It is much cheaper to replace a tip than to put down 10% more chemical.

- **Output volume.** It's usually measured in volume per unit of time (e.g., gallons per minute). General home pest control calls for lower rates; termite pretreats require higher rates. Higher output generally suggests faster treatments but higher chemical costs.

- **Output pattern.** The most popular pest- and weed-control patterns are flat fan and cone/stream. The cone/stream tip delivers a more focused chemical application. The flat-fan tip generally allows a technician to cover a larger area more quickly.

- **Droplet size.** Mosquito fogging uses a tiny droplet size to create a fog that hangs in the air. Smaller droplets can drift to unintended targets, such as a neighbor's yard, kid's toys, pet dishes, etc. Termite pretreats and weed preemergents are at the other extreme and are applied with a large droplet size so the water goes and stays exactly where it's needed.

Two important points about tip selection:

- **Start with the right tip.** This decision is based on your application protocol and should be made after considering all the above.

- **Replace tips regularly.** Brass spray tips wear out at a rate of about 10 percent a year (Source: "Application of Pesticides in Professional Pest Control" by Cecil Paterson and William Robinson of the B&G Equipment Company and Spraying Systems Company). Every year, the tip outputs 10 percent more chemical, which is an involuntary increase of chemical costs. If the spray pattern wears out, the chemical could be applied where it isn't intended. Replacing tips is cheaper than using worn tips. Plastic tips wear out faster; stainless steel tips wear more slowly.

Maintenance

- Inspect tips regularly.

- If needed, clean tips with a mild detergent and a soft bristled brush (an old toothbrush works great). Don't use nails, pins, knives, etc., which will damage the tip.

- Replace tips when the pattern deteriorates or annually, whichever is sooner.

H. Other components: supply hoses, fittings, clamps, valves and quick disconnects.

When purchasing new power spray equipment, most

buyers look only at the most expensive components: engine, pump, tank, reel, etc. Because small parts also can have a big impact on productivity and downtime, it's worth paying attention to these items both when buying new equipment and maintaining existing gear. While these small components might be inexpensive, a worn component or the wrong component in the wrong place can cause considerable safety problems, such as injuries, chemical spills and exposure, or burst hoses spewing chemicals. Examples of actions that ensure small parts don't have a big negative impact are:

- **Supply hoses.** Use the right type of hose in the right place. Use suction hose between the tank and pump because it won't collapse. After the pump, use pressure hose so it doesn't burst.

  Make sure supply hoses are clear of hot and moving parts. Ensure supply hoses don't rub against other components that will wear down the supply hose. Check supply hoses to make sure moving parts or truck vibration aren't causing abnormal wear. If you see this type of wear, replace the hose and wrap the new hose with a larger diameter hose to prevent the same problem from reoccurring.

  The fewer constrictions, fittings, valves, twists and turns in the supply hoses, the easier it will be for the pump to suck and push water and the fewer components there are to fail.

  Inspect hoses periodically for damage, wear, cuts, nicks, sun damage, cracking, etc. In addition to the spray hose, check hoses between tanks, pumps, reels, etc. If one of these hoses bursts while the technician is at the end of 200 feet of spray hose, a large chemical spill will need to be cleaned up.

  Sometimes supply hoses have kinks in them, which impacts system operations, productivity and safety.

Hoses have a usable life and should be replaced periodically. Proactively inspect and replace hoses before they fail.

- **Plumbing fittings.** There are wide variations in the quality of plumbing fittings. For example, fittings can be steel, brass, black pipe, PVC, nylon, etc. Fittings are almost never specified when buying a new rig. The wrong fitting in a critical position can be disastrous. A fitting that's too short, thin or weak can crack under pressure, vibration or torque, resulting in an expensive spill. This risk is magnified in areas of hot or cold temperature extremes or where the sprayer will constantly be driven over bumpy roads. Select fittings that can withstand the product being applied. For example, herbicides and fertilizers will destroy black pipe fittings quickly.

Key Points

- Higher-pressure systems require sturdier, heavier-duty fittings.

- Fittings attached to valves that are turned or hoses that are pulled should be heavier duty to handle the stress. It might make sense to secure the valve or hose to the vehicle or skid so the valve takes the stress instead of the fitting.

- Fittings for larger diameter hoses, such as on tree sprayers or termite pretreat rigs, should be sturdier and longer to handle the weight of the hose.

- Fittings in key or high-risk positions should be heavy

duty to reduce risk. For example, the pickup fitting coming out of the bottom of a tank is critical. If it breaks, the tank will empty. This happened to a local government agency. A cheap plastic fitting on a brand new, weed sprayer broke the first day it was used, creating a 100-gallon chemical spill.

• **Clamps.** Make sure your rig has high-quality clamps that can withstand pressure, wear, abuse, etc. Even new spray rigs can use inferior quality clamps that increase the risk to the spray technician and company. On high-pressure rigs, consider double or triple clamping hoses for extra safety and security.

• **Valves.** A strategically placed valve can be used to reduce the risk of leaks, spills and downtime – and adds only a minimal cost. For example, a valve placed at the hose end before the spray gun reduces the risk of a leaking gun because the technician can shut off the flow, rather than letting the gun leak. A valve before the line strainer (filter) allows a technician to check the filter regardless of the amount of water in the tank. Use heavy-duty, industrial grade valves instead

Herbicides destroyed this black pipe fitting. Be sure to match fittings to the material being applied.

Quality is important throughout the sprayer. A cheap fitting or clamp can lead to a chemical spill.

of cheap valves that are likely to fail. Check the valves to ensure they're functioning properly. Replace worn or damaged valves.

With all these examples, the cost of the valve is small compared to the total cost of the sprayer and potential downtime and chemical spills, which can be prevented.

Suggestions

- Inspect power sprayers for proper valving.

  ➢ Are valves in key places to prevent or reduce spills?
  ➢ Are valves in key places to allow access to critical components (pump, filter, etc.) even when the tank is full?
  ➢ Are valves made from high-quality materials, or were cheaper valves used to save money?

- When purchasing new power sprayers, know what you're getting.

  ➢ Question your vendor to understand what valves are included with the sprayer. Ask about valve quality, location and purpose.
  ➢ Ask spray technicians where they'd like to see shut off valves.

When purchasing a power sprayer, pay attention to all components, not just the expensive ones. This is particularly important with regard to government purchases based on lowest bid. When purchasing spray equipment, government buyers often specify the larger components (engine, pump, reel, tank, etc.), but ignore the small, less-costly components. When not specified, vendors might use lower quality, cheaper parts to cut cost.

Inspect hoses, fittings and clamps periodically to find problems and ensure you and your employees are minimizing risk and increasing safety.

- **Quick disconnects.** Installing quick disconnects (QDs) on a power spray hose can save time and money. QDs are spring-loaded couplings that allow a technician to remove the spray gun from the end of the hose quickly. This offers several advantages compared to the alternative – hard plumbing the gun directly to the hose.

Advantages of QDs include:

- ➤ It's easy to remove a gun for storage, reducing the risk of theft, loss or damage.
- ➤ It's easy to interchange spray guns and tools to select the correct tool for the application.
- ➤ It's easy to remove a spray gun for repair.
- ➤ QDs allow an easy interchange of tools or installation of backup tools should the primary spray gun fail.
- ➤ QDs allow the spray gun to rotate freely on the hose, making the hose easier to handle and putting less stress on the last few feet of hose.

QDs have two parts – the male (nipple) and the female (coupler), which fit together. They come in standard sizes. Most common pest and weed applications require 3/8 inch or 1/2 inch. Larger volume applications, such as termite pretreats, often use larger sizes, e.g., 3/4 inch and 1 inch.

QDs are available in two general styles:

- **Valved QDs** have internal shutoffs that prevent water from passing through the QD when the nipple and coupler are separated. One can remove the gun from the spray hose, and the QD won't allow water to pass, even if the pump is on. Valved QDs can help prevent leaks and spills and allow a technician to remove the spray gun without worrying about leaks. Valved QDs disadvantages are they're heavier and more expensive than unvalved QDs and can be difficult to release when the line is under pressure.

- **Unvalved, or free flow QDs** allow water to pass through unimpeded, whether they're connected or not. They're lighter and less expensive than their valved counterparts, but the spray gun can't be removed from the hose without a spill. We prefer using a brass ball valve in front of an unvalved QD, which overcomes this drawback.

Suggestions for using QDs are:

- **Standardize.** Installing the same size and style QDs on all vehicles and spray tools ensures the correct tool, and backup is always available.

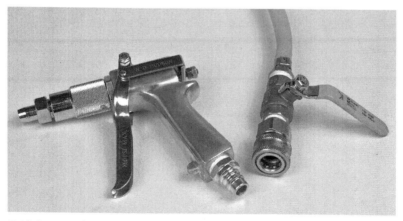

Quick disconnects boost productivity and reduce downtime by helping ensure the correct spray tool is readily available.

- **Periodically inspect QDs** for wear or damage to prevent problems. Make sure the spring mechanism works properly and QDs can be operated easily.

- **Maintenance.** Eventually, the O-ring in the coupler will wear out. Keep a couple of repair kits and backup QD sets available for maintenance.

QDs can help improve technician productivity and reduce downtime. Properly used, the advantages more than offset the small incremental investment of installing them.

I. Agitation

When it comes to spray equipment, it's critical to ensure the product is well mixed. This is particularly true for landscape and golf applications that involve products that aren't water soluble granular fertilizers, for example. Problems can occur if the product isn't mixed well.

- **Incorrect application rates.** If the product isn't mixed well in the tank, the product might be applied unevenly or at an incorrect rate. In either case, the desired results won't be achieved, and money will be wasted on extra product, call backs or fixing undesired results.

- **Tank build up.** If the material isn't mixed well, it will settle to the bottom of the tank. If no action is taken, tank buildup can become severe and expensive to clean.

- **Clogged lines.** If the material isn't mixed properly, it can be sucked into lines and clog downstream components. The first component to clog will be the filter. If the staff is checking the filter frequently, they should be able to identify the problem, which will prevent equipment damage.

If the filter isn't cleaned, the pump could become starved for water, which can result in pump damage. If the pump continues to run dry, it can become a total loss. The material also can clog hoses, fittings and spray tips, which can cause system damage, resulting in downtime and increased equipment repair costs. In some instances, plumbing fittings have been completely clogged and the pump has been completely destroyed. The most common methods of ensuring a good tank mix are:

- **Mechanical agitation.** Mechanical agitation is an effective way to ensure a good tank mix. It's accomplished by turning a series of stainless steel paddles inside the tank. The paddles are attached to a stainless steel shaft that runs through the tank. The shaft is turned by a the gas engine that drives the pump. When the engine is on, the tank is agitated. Properly designed, mechanical agitation provides excellent, continuous agitation. Mechanical agitation isn't feasible with electric-powered sprayers because there's no exposed engine shaft available to drive the agitation. Mechanical agitation must be installed when a system is built. It's usually not feasible to add it retroactively. It's also expensive because all the parts are precision-engineered stainless steel. Eventually, the seals and bearings that allow the shaft to turn will leak and require service. The sprayer will be out of service during the time the mechanical agitation is serviced. Be sure to ask who will service the mechanical agitation and if parts are available.

- **Jet agitation**. Jet agitation is a more commonly used method because of lower purchase and maintenance costs. It involves diverting a portion of the pump's output back into the tank through carefully positioned jet agitation nozzles.

  A couple of important considerations for jet agitation: There must be enough jet nozzles in the tank to stir the entire tank. The nozzles must be positioned to avoid dead spots in the tank. It's also important to make sure none of the agitation nozzles are positioned toward the pickup tube that feeds the pump. The flow from the agitation nozzle can interfere with the pump intake.

  Usually, jet agitation is less costly to install than mechanical agitation. The primary cost of jet agitation is sometimes a larger pump with sufficient output (measured in gallons per minute) to drive the agitation, in addition to the spray hose or boom.

  It's important to calculate accurately to ensure the system has the appropriately size pump. If the pump is too small, spray performance will be unacceptable.

Here are the rules of thumb:

➢ Liquid products require 8 percent of tank volume (in gallons per minute) for jet agitation.

➢ Dry or granular products require 12 percent of tank volume. For example, if one is using a granular fertilizer in a 200-gallon tank, he'll require 24 gallons per minute (12% x 200 gallons = .12 x 200 = 24 gallons) for agitation.

Most agitation nozzles provide a multiplier (usually 3x, 5x or 7x) that increases the effect of the agitation. Said another way, the agitation nozzles reduce the volume of water required for agitation.

Continuing the example above with 3x nozzles, the 24 gpm requirement is reduced to 8 gpm (24 gpm divided by 3). The number of nozzles doesn't affect the calculation. For this example, a pump is required that puts out at least 8 gpm more than is required to drive the boom or spray gun. If the pump output is insufficient to drive the output and agitation, a user won't be able to agitate at the same time he's spraying. Remember, actual output of most pumps will be lower than the manufacturer specification, and that pump output declines with pump age. Include a margin of safety when computing jet agitation requirements. Put a gate valve on the agitation line so the volume of agitation can be adjusted. Sometimes more output is required to the spray hose, so the agitation is turned down. Conversely, sometimes more agitation is required, so the valve is opened completely.

- **Mix tanks**. Mix tanks are separate cone-bottom tanks with dedicated high-volume pumps that mix products into water thats pumped into spray units. Cone tanks are great if users have multiple sprayers and a lot of material to apply. The downside is the expense of a separate unit. Mix tanks usually rely on high-volume centrifugal pumps to churn the material in the tank, which is then drawn out the bottom of the tank and pumped into individual sprayers. The pumps can be gas or electric powered. Some considerations when selecting mix tanks:

  - ➢ Select a high-volume pump for which replacement parts are readily available. Be sure the output at the cone bottom of the tank has an antivortex fitting. Without this fitting, a vortex or whirlpool effect can form, which prevents the adequate flow of material out the bottom of the tank. Be sure the pump and hoses are plumbed with detachable cam fittings so the pump can be used to fill, mix and empty the tank.

- **Premix.** With equipment with insufficient agitation, the best bet might be to premix the material in a bucket of water, then dump it gradually into the tank. If there's a spray hose and gun, use the gun to spray back into the tank to help mix the material.

    To ensure ideal results, review the spray equipment to ensure products are mixed and applied properly. Be sure employees are trained to mix products and look for and identify potential problems before they become problems requiring expensive repairs and significant downtime.

J. Tank pickup line

One feature of power professional spray rigs that doesn't receive much attention is the pickup line, which feeds water from the tank to the pump. It's important to pay attention to the pickup, because if problems occur here, it can significantly affect productivity, downtime, repair expense and chemical spills. Generally speaking, pickup on most pest or weed sprayers can be designed as top pickup or bottom-end pickup.

Top pickup involves a penetration at the top of the tank, with a pickup tube that allows the pump to suck the material from the bottom of the tank. Bottom-end pickup involves a penetration at the bottom-end of the tank, so gravity does much of the work of getting the material toward the pickup. There are pros and cons to both.

- **Top pickup**
  Pro:
  > If the penetration tank fitting leaks, no chemical can spill because the fitting is at the top of the tank.

  Con:
  > If the pickup tube cracks, breaks or becomes clogged, the pump can't suck material causing downtime. If the pump is old or worn, it might have trouble generating enough suction to lift the water up the pickup tube.

- **Bottom end pickup**
  Pro:
  > There's no pickup tube, so there are fewer parts to have problems, and the pump doesn't have to work as hard to draw liquid because gravity is helping.

  Con:
  > If the tank fitting develops a leak, a chemical spill could occur because the fitting is at the bottom of the tank.
  >
  > Our shop usually recommends bottom-end pickup because on the rare occasions when the tank fitting leaks, it usually starts as a tiny leak that can be mitigated easily until the tank is empty and the fitting can be replaced. The benefits of bottom feed far outweigh the small risk of a leak.

- **Other considerations.** For top feed, be sure the bottom of the pickup tube isn't tight against the bottom of the tank or it will clog. Cut a few notches in the bottom of the pickup tube to prevent debris from clogging.

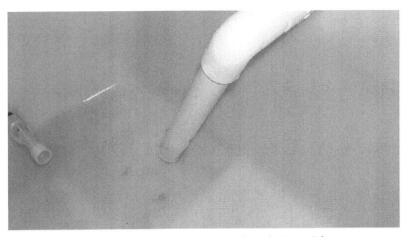

There are several potential pickup tube problems. This tube is too tight to bottom of tank and could become clogged

- **For bottom feed.** Sometimes the tank design prevents the tank fitting from being at the very bottom of the tank, which means the pump can't suck water from below the level of the tank fitting. We recommend installing an elbow fitting inside the tank to allow the pump to empty the tank further.

- **Middle feed.** Middle feed combines the problems of both solutions and should be avoided.

Some of our landscape customers want a sump in the bottom of the tank and the pickup to be at the very bottom of the tank. This allows the tank to be emptied completely, but it adds cost because a frame is required to raise the tank so plumbing can be installed under the tank.

Whichever solution is selected, ensure technicians understand how it works so if problems occur, appropriate actions can be taken to reduce downtime.

K. Filtration: the best way to boost sprayer productivity

Want to boost productivity, improve service and reduce repair expenses? When it comes to pest and weed spray equipment, the most effective means of achieving these results is proper filtration. Filtration removes suspended foreign material – dirt, sand, rocks, trash or anything else that makes its way into the spray tank other than water and chemicals – from water. Filtration is critical to spray professionals because debris wreaks havoc. Debris damages pumps; clogs hoses, guns and tips; and starves pumps of water, causing extensive damage. As much as 50 percent of sprayer repairs are avoidable if proper filtration design and operation is implemented.

- **Design.** Filtration design includes equipment selection, placement and access. Selection should be based on material (chemical) being applied, quality of water, technician compliance and the type of pump. Most power sprayers can get by with one line strainer between the tank and pump.

Sometimes more than one filter is required. This termite pretreat sprayer used an additional filter on the hydrant fill because of poor water quality.

The line strainer refers to the complete unit, which contains a stainless steel filter. The mesh of the filter is important: too fine, and it will clog quickly; too coarse, and debris will pass through the filter to the pump, spray tips, etc. Manufacturers use a number rating to describe filter mesh size. The higher the number, the finer the mesh. For example, a 20 filter is coarser than a 50 filter.

If the water source is poor, use additional filtration. Many termite pretreaters in new home developments rely on water lines filled with debris. Some golf courses fill their sprayers with pond water. For these applications, add extra filtration. Examples include a line strainer on the hydrant fill line, a filter basket in the tank fill well, and/or two line strainers between the tank and pump. In the last situation, the first filter is coarse, and the second is fine – a combination that works well to eliminate most debris.

Some pumps require more filtration than others. Roller pumps are more sensitive to debris and require better filtration than diaphragm pumps.

It's critical the filtration device be located for easy access. It must be easy for the technician to reach and check the filter. The system must be plumbed so the filter can be checked without causing a spill. If the tank is bottom-plumbed and the strainer is below the water level in the tank, install a shut-off valve so the filter can be checked even when the tank is full. Standardize filtration across all vehicles so it easy for technicians to find and check the filter. Standardization helps ensure replacement parts, such as O-rings and screens, are always available.

- **Operation.** Checking and cleaning the filter is the most valuable preventive maintenance task technicians can perform. It's also the easiest. For new equipment, check the filter daily. If there's consistently no debris, consider reducing the frequency. When you determine the appropriate frequency, make it a company policy. Checking the filter too often is better than too seldom. Reinforce the importance of checking and cleaning the filter with spray techs. Supervisors should periodically inspect filters to ensure technicians are paying attention.

- **Maintenance.** Eventually, the filter will become too dirty to clean. When this happens, replace it. Chemicals will eventually swell the gasket in the line strainer, making it impossible to create an airtight seal and cause the pump to suck air. If this happens, replace the gasket. Equip each vehicle with an extra

This filter was heavily clogged with herbicide. The pump was starved for water and was a total loss.

filter and gasket so the technician can perform the repair in the field. This is easy if you've standardized the filtration. Eventually, the line strainer body may crack, causing an air leak. When this happens, replace the entire unit.

L. Storage: Make sure to leave room

Pest-and weed-control equipment storage is a function of vehicle, pest/weed control methodology, tools and employee training (e.g., specialized vs. universal technician, etc.). There might be an ideal solution for a particular company, but I don't believe there's a best solution for the industry.

We won't have a full discussion about toolboxes, but here are a few key points:

> ➤ When buying a power sprayer, don't forget to leave room for the toolbox. Leave enough

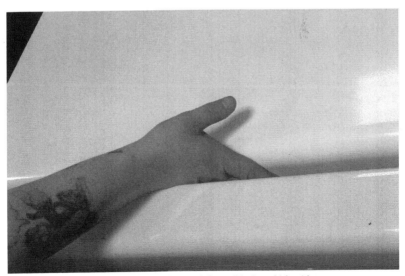

Plan ahead when buying equipment. **Make sure it fits well in the vehicle with room for access. This toolbox is too close to the tailgate and could result in injury.**

clearance for the toolbox lid to open completely without smashing your hand.

➤ Put the most commonly used pest control equipment and supplies in the easiest access locations.

➤ Ensure heavy items are located near the side or rear of the truck to prevent back injuries when lifting.

➤ Store pesticides separately from baits, glue boards and respirators, so these items don't absorb odors.

➤ Secure all equipment, even if it's not in a toolbox. If not secured, equipment such as B&G sprayers, backpack sprayers and ladders can be damaged or become airborne in an accident.

➤ Consider drilling holes in the bottom of the box to allow it to be cleaned with water.

➤ Inspect the connection points of the toolbox to ensure it's fashioned securely to the vehicle.

➤ Standardize equipment, storage methods and locations wherever possible. Standardization makes training, service, spare parts, repairs and inspections easier.

Get ideas from others:

➤ Ask employees what they like and dislike.

➤ Ask equipment suppliers for advice.

➤ Walk the parking lot at industry trade shows and conferences, and observe other vehicles to see other companies' solutions.

M. The truck and power spray equipment

There are many factors to consider when purchasing a truck for pest or weed control. How does your desired power spray equipment configuration work in your truck? Many new trucks have features that affect installation and power spray equipment use. There are fewer issues when installing new equipment because there's more flexibility when selecting and locating new equipment versus existing equipment.

- **Payload capacity.** The truck must be able to haul equipment safely. The heaviest component is the chemical tank when it's full of water. Water weighs about 8.4 pounds per gallon. Too big a truck means higher up-front cost, higher insurance and fuel bills.

Be sure there's room under the bed to bolt the sprayer down where you want it to go.

Too small a truck can mean increased expenses for tires, brakes and transmission repairs.

- **Truck bed size.** Obviously, the bed must be big enough to hold equipment in the configuration required. It's not a good idea to assume equipment that fits in an old truck will fit in the current year make and model of the same truck. Manufacturers change bed dimensions.

- **Truck bed depth.** Manufacturers sometimes change the depth of truck beds. For example, Ford's F150 beds are deeper than they were a few years ago. This can impact a technician's access to the engine pull start, hose reel handles or electric switches.

- **Bed construction.** Some smaller trucks have beds made entirely of plastic. Plastic ribs on the underside of the bed provide bed strength. More care is required when fastening equipment to the plastic bed to ensure stability and strength. Piercing a rib can impact bed strength.

- **Gas tank.** The size, location and position of gas tanks on some models has changed. For some smaller trucks, it's not possible to access the bed above the gas tank. This can impact installation. In these situations, it might not be possible to install a water tank directly above the gas tank because there's no access to tighten bolts. In this case, the water tank must be mounted to a metal frame, which allows more flexibility in bolt location.

- **Other below bed obstructions.** Sometimes there's something under the bed that prevents equipment installation in a specific location. Examples include structural steel members and an exhaust system. In these instances, shift the spray equipment to a location where it can be bolted down safely.

- **Clearance.** Ground clearance in some smaller vehicles is reduced. Getting under the truck to tighten bolts or wire electrical spray components can be more difficult. These trucks require a lift to gain access for installation.

- **Electrical system.** The electrical system of many vehicles has becoming more complex. Many vehicles have computer controlled electrical systems that can make wiring more complex and time consuming.

- **None of these issues are showstoppers.** They're factors to consider for layout, installation, time and budgeting when installing equipment.

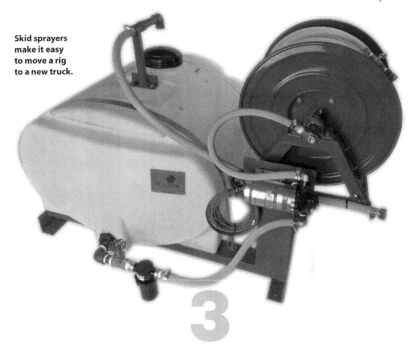

Skid sprayers make it easy to move a rig to a new truck.

POWER SPRAY EQUIPMENT DESIGN AND LAYOUT

A. Skid vs. component vs. trailer mount

There numerous ways to mount power spray equipment in a vehicle. The most common are skid, component and trailer mounts. Skid mount is attaching all the sprayer components on a metal (usually steel or aluminum) frame. The frame then is bolted to the vehicle. Component mount is bolting all the components individually to the vehicle. Trailer mount means mounting components on a trailer that's towed behind a technician's truck. Here are the pros and cons of each.

- **Skid mount**
  Pros
  - ➤ **Easy to install.** Just bolt the skid to the vehicle.
  - ➤ **The skid provides numerous places to bolt the sprayer**, which is helpful in compact pickup trucks

where access under the bed is limited.

➢ **With only one unit, it's easier to remove from the vehicle** if the vehicle is to be used for another purpose, replaced or down for service.

➢ **Supports company equipment standardization** because most equipment vendors build standard skid sprayers

Cons

➢ **The frame adds cost and weight.**

➢ **Most companies don't frequently move skids** in and out of trucks, so the easy-to-move benefit isn't that valuable.

➢ **The equipment goes where the manufacturer puts it.** Particularly on standard spray skids, the owner or operator of the equipment has no input on where the components are mounted. This can affect access for use and maintenance.

➢ **Just because equipment fits in the truck**, doesn't mean it will fit – or work well – when moved to another truck.

Component mount provides more flexibility when locating sprayer components

- **Component mount**

  Pros

  ➢ **Saves money and weight** because there's no skid to buy.

  ➢ **More flexibility when locating components** where they're convenient for operation and maintenance and to make room for other equipment, e.g., toolbox.

  ➢ **Increases chances equipment will fit** when moving it to a new truck.

  ➢ **Strongly recommended for flatbed and large trucks** to improve equipment access by moving equipment to the truck sides.

  Cons

  ➢ **Takes longer to install** because all components (tank, pump, motor, reel) must be bolted down individually.

  ➢ **Takes longer to move to a different vehicle** because each component must be removed and reinstalled in new vehicle.

  ➢ **Can be difficult to do in smaller vehicles.** Gas tank, structural members and other components can make it difficult to bolt components in their desired locations.

- **Trailer mount**

  Pros

  ➢ **Flexibility.** Sprayers in a truck have no flexibility. If the truck needs service or is in an accident, the sprayer is unavailable. A sprayer in a trailer can be used by multiple vehicles or technicians.

  ➢ **Personal vehicle.** For owner/operators, this is important. It took months to get reservations at the best restaurant in town. You put on your best duds and pick up your date. Do you want to arrive in a truck hauling a stinky pest control spray rig? If the sprayer is mounted in a trailer, you can leave it behind so you can strut your stuff.

➢ **Space.** Trailers often can hold larger water tanks than a pickup truck, which enables one to perform more and larger jobs. The trailer dramatically increases the size and volume of equipment one can carry on a route.

➢ **Backup.** A spray trailer makes an ideal backup when another sprayer is down.

➢ **Equipment location.** There's more flexibility in equipment location in a trailer. In a pickup truck, numerous constraints (gas tank, wheel wells, structural members under the bed) can make it difficult to place equipment exactly where one wants it.

Cons

➢ **Safety.** Hauling a 3,000-pound spray trailer in traffic causes safety concerns. Stopping distances increase. Ability to maneuver the vehicle is reduced. Safety is less of a concern when the company owner is

A 225-gallon trailer sprayer component mount

driving compared to a 21-year-old employee who's driving and texting his girlfriend at the same time.
➢ **Important.** Install equipment on the trailer so the trailer is slightly tongue heavy, which usually means placing the water tank over, then slightly forward, of the axle.
➢ **Important.** Contact your insurance agent before buying a trailer to identify insurance-related issues.
➢ **Maneuverability.** It's more difficult to maneuver a vehicle with a spray trailer behind it.
➢ **Cost.** The trailer is an additional cost compared to putting the sprayer in a truck.
➢ **Storage.** Finding additional space to store the trailer can be problematic.
➢ **Theft.** Trailers are targets for thieves. Plenty of trailers are stolen, even when chained to a lamppost.

B. Spray equipment: design for access

Power spray equipment must be designed for easy access by the spray and maintenance technicians. The spray tech will be using the equipment every day. The sprayer must be easy to use and support the tech's productivity. If key components are difficult to reach or use, the equipment is hindering, rather than helping, productivity. For example, is it easy to pull start the engine? Is it easy for the tech to check and clean the filter? Is it easy to crank the hose reel? These are the types of questions to think about before the sprayer is purchased and installed.

All spray equipment needs maintenance. The sprayer must be designed so maintenance is relatively easy. Is should be easy to change the engine oil and remove the pump so it can be rebuilt. Bad design means repairs will take longer than necessary, resulting in more downtime and costly repairs.

Remember, equipment breaks down during the busy season, when downtime hurts the most.

Other features of effective and efficient design are:

- **Designed for hard use.** Put heavy-duty components in key places that can stand up to pressure, harsh chemicals, temperature extremes and long operating hours.

- **Ease of cleaning.** Most technicians don't like to clean their equipment. If it's difficult to clean, they won't do it. Equipment that's regularly cleaned has fewer problems than filthy equipment.

- **Use heavy-duty valves to mitigate spills.** This is covered in the safety section.

Ensure key components are accessible. This engine start isn't accessible

- **Put heavy items by the tailgate.** Equipment such as a backpack sprayer, should be lifted out of the vehicle at the rear of the truck so technicians can ease the equipment out on the lowered tailgate. Lifting items over the side of the truck stresses one's back.

- **Commonly used items are easiest to reach.** Ensure items used every day are near the side or rear of the vehicle and are unobstructed for easy access. A technician shouldn't have to spend time reaching or searching for everyday items.

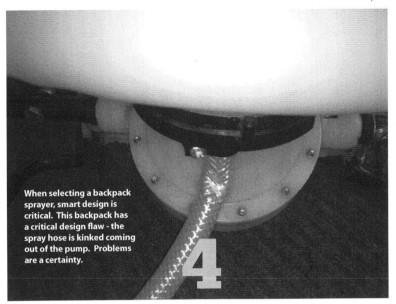

When selecting a backpack sprayer, smart design is critical. This backpack has a critical design flaw - the spray hose is kinked coming out of the pump. Problems are a certainty.

MANUAL SPRAYERS: START WITH THE RIGHT EQUIPMENT

Backpacks and compressed air manual sprayers are important tools in a spray tech's arsenal.

A. Selection – start with the right equipment

- **Standardize.** If all your backpacks and manual sprayers are the same, everything is easier: training, operation, maintenance and parts inventory. Standardization is one reason Southwest Airlines, which flies only 737s, makes money when other airlines lose money.

- **Quality.** Select a quality product. For example, the spray valve (i.e., the spray gun) should be well built with quality materials, such as brass or steel, not plastic. The backpack must be well-built. If the backpack looks flimsy, it probably is, so don't buy it.

- **Serviceability.** If you can't service the sprayer, it's a throwaway. The pump must be easily accessible for cleaning and service. The backpack's filter must be easy to access and clean. If you can't clean the filter, the backpack won't last.

- **Repair parts.** Ensure repair parts are available. If not, the sprayer is a throwaway. Don't buy it.

- **Multiple tips.** Are multiple spray tips available for the backpack? If not, the backpack can be used only one way, which limits its value.

B. Use: Smart use extends product life

- **Check it out.** Technicians should check their equipment quickly before leaving their starting point (home or office). This can be as simple as a visual inspection, pressurizing the unit, and a spray to ensure proper operation. If you don't want to discharge the product, techs can team up and spray into each other's sprayer. If you're going to have a problem, have it where and when you can do something about it, rather than in the field.

- **Make sure it's secure.** Don't drive off until you're certain the backpack is secure in the vehicle and will stay in place if there's a sudden stop, traffic accident, etc.

- **Take it easy.** Make sure technicians aren't overpressurizing sprayers, which damages equipment, leading to downtime, missed appointments and increased repair expenses. If the backpack isn't spraying, pumping it up will break it. It's easy to turn a $3.00 O-ring replacement into a $50 rebuild.

- **Take the pressure off.** There will be longer life and fewer problems from your manual spray equipment if your technicians release the pressure in their unit. Certainly, the pressure should be released at the end of the day and optimally at the end of each stop. Leaving your sprayer under pressure for an extended time will reduce the life of components such as hoses, gaskets and O-rings. Just like your body, which needs recreation or relaxation to relieve the stress of the workday, your sprayer needs relief or something will blow. Relieving pressure also reduces the risk of freeze damage.

- **Prevent freeze damage.** Don't expose the backpack to freezing temperatures. If this is unavoidable, release the pressure and drain all water from spray valve, hoses, etc.

- **It's a spray wand, not a crowbar.** Use the sprayer the way it's supposed to be used. Don't use the wand to open gates or push obstacles out of the way.

- **Ensure backpack users report problems.** Employees will ignore problems and keep using sprayers. Problems always become worse when ignored.

Proper use extends equipment life. This spray wand was used as a crowbar.

C. Maintenance: Waiting for problems is expensive

Here are the critical maintenance factors for hand sprayers and backpacks:

Replacing this worn out lid gasket will prevent a chemical spill. Replace worn parts before spills occur.

- **Clean the filter.** This is the easiest and most impactful maintenance task you can do to reduce problems and extend sprayer life. Check the filter every day.

- **Clean out the backpack.** Debris and chemicals can build up in the tank, pump, hoses and tips. Triple rinse the tank periodically, and flush the sprayer with clean water.

- **Clean tips.** Use an old toothbrush and mild dish soap. Don't use needles or any other metal objects that will damage the tip.

- **Replace worn tips.** Worn tips apply more product, which costs money.

- **Preventive maintenance (PM).** Don't wait for your sprayer to fail and cause down-time. Perform required preventive maintenance, which saves money. At the end of the season, tear down the backpack, thoroughly clean all components, and replace O-rings and worn parts.

- **Training.** Make sure employees understand proper use and maintenance. Periodically review proper procedures because employees forget or look for shortcuts that will cost money.

- **Emergency repair kit.** Some parts, such as O-rings and gaskets, can be replaced easily in the field. Prepare a small emergency repair kit for each technician so they can perform simple repairs and continue their route.

- **Eyes open.** Despite the best training, technicians don't always follow company procedures. Conduct ride-alongs to observe how employees use equipment in the field. Conduct truck inspections to ensure equipment is well maintained.

- **Proper storage.** Make sure trucks are set up to provide secure sprayer storage. We often see damage caused by sprayers bouncing around, being stepped on or damaged by other loose equipment. Supervisors should inspect vehicles for proper storage.

- **Report it.** Make sure technicians are comfortable reporting problems. Too many times we see techs working with equipment that needs service. Instead of asking for help, they push the equipment past the breaking point, turning a small repair into a significant rebuild.

- **Tracking.** Track equipment failures to know which parts are failing, which replacement parts should be stocked or which equipment isn't appropriate for your service program. Track failures by technician to identify training opportunities.

  Hand sprayers and backpacks are critical to a company's success. Invest the time to train employees and properly maintain equipment. Follow up to ensure it's done, which will keep employees productive and on schedule, customers happy and repair expenses to a minimum.

This ladder isn't secured. Hitting a bump could result in damaged spray equipment or an airborne ladder.

Clean equipment, including the tank to prevent chemical exposure and present a professional image.

5

SPRAY EQUIPMENT POLICIES FOR SAFETY, SAVINGS AND PRODUCTIVITY

Purchasing the right spray equipment and installing it in a vehicle are the first steps. Once one has the equipment, proper operation is important to ensure effective results, efficient productivity, and limited downtime and repair expenses. The following are suggestions for operating procedures that will help boost productivity and reduce downtime.

A. Safety: Not just a good idea, it's a great investment

Lack of attention to safety has huge financial implications: increased expenses (workers comp, clean ups, medical bills, lawsuits, repairs, etc.), lost productivity, employee turnover, customer impacts and bad publicity.

Safety considerations for spray professionals are:

- **Vehicle load security.** Equipment that's not secure poses a risk to:

  - ➤ **The driver.** Flying equipment could injure the driver or interfere with his ability to control the vehicle.
  - ➤ **Other people on the road.** Equipment flying out of a vehicle moving 60 miles an hour will cause damage if it hits someone or something. Can you say lawsuit?
  - ➤ **The equipment.** Loose equipment causes damage to itself or other equipment on the vehicle. Unsecured equipment causes avoidable problems. There are better ways to spend your money than repairing unnecessarily damaged equipment.

Here are key points to keep in mind.

- Just because it's in the truck, don't assume it's secure.

- Just because it was secured five years ago when you installed it, doesn't mean it's secure today.

- Just because it's secure at 25 miles per hour under normal driving conditions doesn't mean it will be secure in an emergency situation, such as collisions, hard stops, and evasive maneuvers to avoid accidents.

Train technicians to check their load before starting their route. A minute or two can save money, and prevent injuries, downtime and lawsuits.

Small equipment should be placed in security racks or secured otherwise. These racks also help prevent theft. We don't recommend bungee cords, but they're better than nothing. Cramming stuff together isn't securing it. Small equipment (backpack sprayers, line trimmers) should be checked by the technician every day to ensure it's secure. Large equipment that's bolted to the vehicle (power spray rigs, toolboxes, etc.) should be checked periodically.

For example:

- **Tool box.** Tool boxes are usually bolted through the bottom of the tool box to the truck. Inspect for rust, fatigue, or other wear around the bolts. If the material around the bolts is weak, in the event of a crash, the box might break loose.

- **Spray rig.** Is it securely bolted to the truck? Are bolts intact and nuts tight? Are the correct fasteners used (stainless steel bolts won't corrode and nylock nuts are unlikely to loosen)?

- **Spray tank.** Are tank straps snug and secure, or loose and worn?

Checking small equipment should be the tech's daily responsibility. Checking large equipment should be the company's responsibility. Inspect regularly. For example, check the large equipment during the regularly scheduled vehicle oil changes.

Supervisors should spot check vehicles to ensure employees are securing their equipment.

We never expect problems to occur, but they do. Be prepared. Conduct periodic inspections to ensure the company and employees are as safe as possible to protect people, property and business.

Properly sized load

- It's critical the load is properly sized for the vehicle.

There has been a trend toward smaller vehicles to reduce vehicle and fuel costs. This is fine as long as the load carried is appropriate to the vehicle. Here's an example of a problem: A company has a 100-gallon sprayer in a full-size truck. The company downsizes to a compact pickup to save on vehicle and gas costs. One hundred gallons is too large a load for a compact pickup. The weight of the load will make it difficult to stop the vehicle and will affect handling, such as having to swerve to avoid a hazard. Additionally, the oversized load will increase repair expenses (brakes, tires, suspension and transmission) and reduce the expected gas mileage savings from switching to the smaller vehicle.

Stable load

In addition to a properly sized load, it's critical the load be stable. Consider these questions:

- Is the load evenly balanced to ensure stable control and even wear on tires and brakes?

- Will the load shift in the event of a sudden turn or stop?

- Will the water in the tank surge when the brakes are applied making it difficult to control the vehicle? If so, add tank baffles to the water tank to reduce the impact of water surge.

Visibility

- Does the equipment obstruct the driver's view of the road behind and to the sides of the vehicle? If so, what can be done to improve visibility?

Cuts, abrasions, hot, moving, rough/rust, tight, overhang, bangs

- Are there any places where the technician can receive an injury from equipment that's hot, sharp, rusted or moving? Be sure these areas are protected so the technician can't inadvertently injure a hand.

- Is equipment overhanging the vehicle, creating bump hazards? Examples include hose reels hanging over the side of the vehicle and trailer hitches that are a pain in the shin. Inspect equipment and vehicle for these hazards.

- Supervisors should ride along with technicians periodically and use the equipment. This will identify hazards and other opportunities for improving equipment selection, design and layout.

Easy up and down into truck, enough room to walk

- On flat-bed trucks, a technician must often climb up onto the bed to access equipment and add chemicals to the tank. Are there steps with nonslip tape and grab bars to ensure employees can get up and down safely? Once on the bed, is there room for the employee to do what needs to be done? For example, an employee stepping over a hot engine isn't a good idea. Plan equipment placement and spacing before buying equipment and vehicle to ensure there's sufficient space.

Clean it easily

- Has equipment been designed so it can be cleaned easily to remove chemical spills and buildup on the equipment and vehicle? Chemicals on equipment and vehicles is unsafe for the operator and can be perceived by the public as a lack of concern about safety.

B. Proper valving prevents spills and other problems

The proper use of shut-off valves, usually ball or gate valves, helps reduce the risk and severity of chemical spills. Unfortunately, because of the increased cost, valves aren't always installed where they should be. The incremental cost of a properly placed valve is minimal compared to the long-term benefit of smaller chemical spills and reduced repair expenses.

Here's an example of poor or nonexisting valve usage.

- **Photo 1** shows a tank penetration at the bottom, with no shut off valve, only a cheap plastic elbow fitting, which is exposed to harsh chemicals, hard use and extreme  weather. If or when the fitting cracks, there's no way to shut off the flow of water. The entire tank contents will spill.

- **Photo 2** shows a gate valve that can be shut off when there's a problem. Another benefit of good valving is the ability to shut off water flow to a key component to allow servicing  without having to wait for the tank to be empty. In this case, by closing the gate valve, the filter can be checked even when the tank is full. Smart valve design will reduce downtime and repair expenses.

- **Photo 3** shows the plumbing under a 200-gallon spray trailer. The manufacturer used a low-cost PVC ball valve under the trailer. There are a couple of problems with this design. First, this is no place for a cheap plastic valve. If a rock kicked up off the street cracks the valve, there's no way to stop the spill. There's too much cheap plastic between the tank and the valve, which means there are more parts to break and more places for the sprayer to leak. A crack in any fitting between the tank and the valve can't be shut off. Don't use cheap fittings in key places (or anywhere for that matter). Install shut off valves as close to the water source as possible to reduce spill risk.

- **Photo 4** shows how a valve can be used to help prevent spills. There's a ball valve in front of the spray gun. All spray guns have rubber O-rings that will leak eventually. The strategic placement of a shut-off valve can help reduce the impact of this type of leak.

In all these examples, the cost of the valve is minimual when compared to the total cost of the sprayer and the cost of downtime and chemical spills that can be prevented.

Suggestions:

- Inspect power sprayers for proper valving. Are valves in key places to prevent or reduce spills?

- Will the valves allow access to critical components, such as the pump and filter, even when the tank is full?

- Are valves made from high-quality materials, or were cheaper valves used to save money?

When purchasing new power sprayers, know what you're buying. Ask your vendor question so you understand what valves are included with the sprayer. Ask about valve quality, location and purpose.

Spray technicians use equipment every day. Ask them where they would like to see shut-off valves.

A few minutes spent examining your equipment to prepare for and anticipate problems will save time and money.

C. Preventive maintenance isn't optional

Harsh chemicals, extreme temperatures, long operating hours, less-than-gentle handling by technicians, age and wear will take their toll on equipment. A preventive maintenance (PM) program will reduce equipment expenses and employee downtime.

General guidelines:

- Consult equipment owner's manuals, or contact your equipment provider for proper operating procedures and maintenance schedules. A lack of proper maintenance might void manufacturer's warranties.

- Train your staff on the proper use of equipment. To get done quickly, technicians often run motors and pumps too fast and at too high an operating pressure, which will reduce equipment life.

- Technicians don't check equipment before starting it up. Instruct technicians to check line strainers (filters), belts and hoses before starting equipment. Teach them to identify problems before they occur.

- Train technicians to report problems instead of just ignoring them. If the pump sounds like it has a problem, it probably does. It's cheaper to find and fix problems early.

- Track damage, repairs and problems by truck, technician and part to identify problems and training opportunities.

- Instruct your equipment provider to install the equipment so it's easily accessible for maintenance and repairs. If equipment isn't easy to service, it's less likely to be serviced.

Create a PM program based on your equipment, technicians, use and organization's operating philosophy. If maintaining productivity and avoiding cancelled stops are top priorities, your program might call for replacing certain components more frequently or at specified intervals, rather than replacing worn or failed parts. To ensure you don't miss anything, take a structured approach to developing your PM program. The suggestions below follow the flow of water from tank through filter, pump, hose and gun.

Here are some highlights to get you started:

- **Tank.** Clean the tank periodically to prevent chemical buildup and debris, which will clog lines and starve the pump. Most pumps will sustain significant damage if run dry for more than a brief time.

- **Line strainer.** Check and clean your line strainer (filter) to prevent debris from getting into the pump. When you can no longer rinse the filter, replace it. Replace the filter O-ring periodically before it swells and no longer creates an airtight seal.

- **Pump.** Service the pump according to manufacturer specifications. Your equipment provider stocks pump repair kits. Service your pump just before or just after your busy season to be sure the pump is ready for next season. If you wait for your pump to fail before servicing it, you can expect longer downtime and more costly repairs.

- **Engine.** Service the engine according to manufacturer specifications. Like the engine in your personal vehicle, changing engine oil is the best thing you can do to extend engine life. Periodic tune-ups (oil, spark plug, air filter) can keep your engine running and your technicians productive. Inspect and replace the pull cord before it breaks. Inspect belts for wear.

- **Hose reel.** Service the hose reel swivel periodically to prevent leaks. Check the reel tensioner and locking pin for wear.

- **Spray gun.** Spray guns can be rebuilt with repair kits available from your equipment provider. Servicing the spray gun will help reduce chemical spills and technician chemical exposure.

- **Check hoses.** Check the spray hose and all supply hoses for excessive wear and damage. Check clamps and connections to ensure a good fit and an airtight seal. Check any O-rings, gaskets, washers, etc. Failure to do so can result in large spills, especially if the technician is at the far end of 200 feet of hose when the leak occurs.

- **Worn tips cost you money.** Equipment experts report*** the brass spray tip on a 1-gallon compressed air sprayer experiences 10-percent nozzle wear each year, which means after one year, your sprayer is putting out 10-percent more chemical than it did the year before. What does this mean to the typical company? Each year your chemical costs increase 10-percent. The nozzle wears out at 10-percent per year, so the situation worsens over time. Unless you can train your technician to walk 10-percent faster each year, your profitability will decline. It's cheaper to replace your tip every year than to buy 10-percent more chemical.

Clean your tip with a soft bristle brush and mild detergent. Using metal, such as knife or pin, will damage the tip and spray pattern. Inspect and replace gaskets and O-rings as needed.

***Source: Application of Pesticides in Professional Pest Control, By Cecil Paterson and William Robinson, B&G Equipment Company, Spraying Systems Company.

D. Clean it out to prevent problems

Don't wait until the busy season to realize you haven't done your maintenance. Use slow periods to get spray equipment in fighting shape for the long hours and hard use it will undoubtedly endure. Taking a little time to prepare will reduce downtime during the critical busy season, and will reduce equipment repair expense by fixing small problems before they become big ones.

The first thing to do is give your tank a thorough cleaning.

Tanks often experience a buildup of chemical residue caused by pesticides falling out of suspension and accumulating on the bottom of the tank.

This causes various problems:

- The buildup can affect the concentration of the material you're applying. For example, if the water in the tank is low and some of the residue came free, you could be applying material at rates higher than the label. Alternatively, you could be inadvertently applying a different chemical from an earlier mix.

- When residue comes free, it clogs filters, hoses, guns and tips. All of these outcomes are negative and will affect equipment availability, technician productivity and repair expenses. Clogged equipment will cause your technician to lose time and could potentially destroy the pump.

- The cleanout process will remove other dirt, rock and debris that accumulate in the tank, which will play havoc with downstream components.

Here are tips for cleaning out a tank:

- Empty the tank as much as possible without running the pump dry.

- Fill the tank with clean water, and run it through the system. Remove the spray gun so it doesn't clog. Periodically check the filter to be sure it doesn't clog. Be sure to follow all applicable laws when dealing with the rinsate. If you don't have a good place to spray the rinsate, spray it into another tank on a different truck.

- Add clean water to the tank. Don't fill the tank. Add just enough water to feed the pump and fill the hose. Most of the tank should be visible. Turn up the pressure on the system, and use the spray gun to pressure wash the inside of the tank. Add more water, then spray the rinsate out as above.

- Fill the tank with water and add tank cleaner, which is available from a chemical supplier. Most of these products use 1 pound of tank cleaner per 100 gallons of tank volume. Put the spray hose end into the tank, and let the system circulate the tank cleaner per the label directions. This will remove any remaining chemical residue. Properly dispose of the tank cleaner rinsate.

- Run another tank of clean water through the system to remove any remaining tank cleaner.

- There might be debris remaining in the tank after you've finished the cleanout. This could be stones, bottle caps, etc. Manually remove this debris so it doesn't cause problems later. If the filter is at the low point in the system, it might be easiest to remove the filter, then use a garden hose to wash debris out of the tank, then out through the filter.

- Finally, check and clean the filter to ensure it's free of debris and ready for the busy season.

A clean tank is a good tank. A little effort will be repaid in reduced downtime and fewer, less expensive equipment repairs. Spend time now preparing the equipment so it can contribute to the company's bottom line this summer.

E. Preflight checklist: Save time and money, serve customers

Every pilot goes through a preflight checklist before flying his plane. The checklist helps a pilot find problems on the ground, where they can be more easily and safely. Professional spray technicians should do the same.

Before getting into the truck and heading to the first stop, spend a few minutes checking equipment. This saves time and money, prevents downtime that impacts productivity and profitability, and hinders timely service to customers.

If you're going to have an equipment problem, you're better off having the problem at the office (or at home if the vehicle is taken home), rather than in the field. At the office, you're better prepared to make a repair, clean up a chemical spill, find a replacement part, substitute a piece of equipment, or make a management decision about how best to proceed. In the field, repairs are more difficult, time consuming and expensive, and the impact of a chemical spill can be disastrous.

Create a custom preflight checklist based on the company's truck and equipment. (See Appendix D for a sample.)

Following are ideas to get started on a checklist:

Manual equipment (hand sprayers and backpacks)
➢ Is there water under the sprayer?
➢ Is there any visible damage?
➢ Pump up the sprayer.

Does the sprayer hold pressure?
➢ Are there any leaks?
➢ Does the sprayer spray properly?
➢ Does the sprayer shut off properly?
➢ Is the spray pattern intact?

Power equipment
- ➤ Check the filter. Clean it, if necessary.
- ➤ Check the O-ring for swelling, which can prevent an airtight seal.
- ➤ Pull 20 to 30 feet of hose off your reel and inspect for wear. Most hose leaks occur here.

Gas rig
- ➤ Check to ensure engine has gas and oil.
- ➤ Inspect pull cord for wear.
- ➤ Inspect belts for wear.
- ➤ Ensure there's water in the tank, so the pump isn't damaged by running dry.
- ➤ Start the rig, and let it build pressure.
- ➤ Check the pressure gauge for proper operating range.
- ➤ Listen to pump and motor for abnormal noises.
- ➤ Inspect all hoses.
- ➤ Check pump for leaks
- ➤ Check all fittings and clamps for leaks.
- ➤ Check tank output fitting for leak.
- ➤ Check hose reel swivel for leaks.
- ➤ Check spray gun for leaks.
- ➤ Use the gun to spray material back into tank. Observe the system for proper operation.
- ➤ Rewind the hose on the reel to test the reel for proper operation.
- ➤ Test electrical components, such as the pump and rewind hose reel, for proper operation.

Other equipment and supplies
- ➤ Ensure there's enough extra gas for the day's stops.
- ➤ Ensure there's enough chemicals for the day's stops.
- ➤ Ensure label/MSDS for the products is on the truck.
- ➤ Ensure there's enough supplies for the day's stops.
- ➤ Ensure proper PPE (personal protective equipment) is on the truck.

> ➤ Ensure there's spill-control supplies on the truck.
> ➤ Ensure the required equipment is on the truck.

Add items to the checklist appropriate for your company. Technicians should report any problems or exceptions they find to their supervisor, who should have a vehicle inspection checklist that includes all the items on the technician checklist plus additional items critical to the company's success.

A few minutes in the morning spent checking equipment, will ensure productivity the entire day.

F. Spray equipment: ignoring problems isn't a strategy

Many spray-equipment problems are significantly worse than they appear to be. In too many instances, spray techs ignore problems hoping they'll go away. As a colleague once told me, hope isn't a strategy.

Much like the slow drip of your kitchen faucet, spray equipment problems always worsen. They don't get better or go away. Small problems inevitably become big problems, which cost more and take longer to fix. Another spray equipment caveat: Water (or oil or any other fluid) that's anywhere it's not supposed to be is always a problem and shouldn't be ignored.

Common problems that get worse with time are:

- **Backpack and compressed air sprayers.**
  Leaks, lack of pressure and other small problems become rebuilds because a tech ignored the problem or used force on a sensitive piece of equipment.

- **Spray pumps.** Most power spray pumps tell the operator the pump requires attention.

For example, gear and roller pumps will leak. Diaphragm pumps have a reservoir that shows the oil has turned a milky white. In each of these cases, if the pump is serviced promptly, a repair kit is usually all that's required. If the problem is ignored, the pump can be a complete loss.

- **Engines** (or any piece of equipment) leaking oil (or other fluids) is a problem and must be dealt with promptly.

- **Hoses, fittings, O-rings and gasket problems** often begin with a slow leak. If ignored, leaks become considerable problems, resulting in significant chemical spills and downtime.

Easy steps to take to prevent these problems are:

- Train technicians regularly to explain proper equipment operation techniques and trouble signs.

- Encourage technicians to report, rather than live with, spray equipment problems.

- Supervisors and managers should spot check trucks and test equipment.

- Regularly clean backpacks and compressed air sprayers to prevent debris from damaging systems.

- Regularly check and clean filters to prevent system damage.

- Perform preventive maintenance on equipment to prevent problems.

These simple steps will reduce equipment problems, repair expense, downtime and missed appointments. Employees, managers, owners and customers will appreciate the effort.

G. Pressure problems that will ruin the day

- **Don't overpressurize.** Pressure is good. Without it, most power and manual sprayers won't work. But too much pressure decreases sprayer life. Here's an interesting observation. When we build a new gas-powered pest spray rig, we install it, test it and send it out at 75 to 100 psi. When spray rigs come into our shop for service, the rigs are often set at 150 psi or higher. The pressure isn't magically increased by a pressure fairy. Pest control technicians turn up the pressure to finish jobs faster. Higher pressure shortens the life of pump, hoses, fittings and guns. Chemical spills will be more dangerous if a component bursts at higher pressure. Higher pressure can affect spray droplet size and cause spray drift. Make sure techs are operating pest control power sprayers at the recommended pressure.

Technicians often spray at higher-than-recommended pressure to finish a job faster.

- **Release the pressure.** Another way to reduce spray equipment problems is to release the pressure. Release pressure on the (power or manual) sprayer after each stop by squeezing the spray gun handle to let the pressure drop in the line. The power sprayer must be turned off, and the manual sprayer must not be pumped up. If spraying extra chemicals is problematic, open the lid of the sprayer tank and spray the product back into the tank.

  Releasing the pressure in the sprayer extends the life of hoses, O-rings and gaskets. We used to suggest releasing the pressure at the end of the day, but technicians forget and sprayers end up stored under pressure all night. It's better to train the technicians to release the pressure at the end of each stop. Temperatures on trucks are higher than ambient temperatures, so the pressure in the system will increase if not released. Releasing the pressure also reduces the chance of freeze damage should a deep freeze occur. If the sprayer is stored under pressure and the temperature drops, the ice will expand and break the weakest link in the system.

H. Emergency repair kits: problems will occur, so be ready

Spray equipment breakdowns can wreak havoc on schedules, impact customers and hinder company profitability. Yet, with planning, some downtime can be avoided. Here's one simple tip: Keep easy-to-replace parts in each truck so minor repairs can be

A well equiped emergency repair kit will reduce downtime and boost productivity

completed in the field. A repair in the field avoids a trip to the repair shop and enables the technician to complete the scheduled stops without customer impact.

All spray equipment wears out, and parts need to be replaced. Buy these parts in advance because you might as well have them when and where you need them. Ideas for parts for your emergency repair kit are:

Manual sprayers:

- **Compressed air sprayers.** Rubber parts swell or wear out because of exposure to pesticides. (Note: Some of the natural, botanical products are even tougher on rubber.) Keep parts such as check valves, lid gaskets, tips and tip O-rings in the kit.

- **Backpack sprayers.** Spray tips, O-rings, filters, lid gaskets tips and check valves are parts that wear out and can be easy to replace.

Power sprayers:

- **Line strainer/filter.** The filter is the source of much trouble, so this is probably the most important part of your emergency repair kit. Include the filter O-ring and the steel screen.

- **Spray guns.** Some commonly used pest control spray guns will leak when O-rings swell. Many of these O-rings are easy to change in the field. Eventually spray tips become clogged or wear out, so keep a replacement in the kit. Some guns are connected to spray hoses with garden-hose fittings. The garden-hose washers in these fittings are replaced easily.

- **Pumps.** Some spray pumps use parts that can be replaced easily in the field. Dampner diaphragms are a common source of trouble on diaphragm pumps. A wrench can be used to gently tighten a leaking gear pump. An extra fuse can get a 12-volt pump or electric hose reel back in service in minutes.

- **Engine.** Changing a bad belt on a gas engine is an easy repair to make on your power spray rig.

- **Spray hose.** Spray hose is dragged across rocks and around building corners and trees. This wear can cause downtime and spills that need to be cleaned up. Create a temporary hose repair kit with a knife, screwdriver, two clamps and hose mender. These parts are available from spray equipment providers. The repair will enable a technician to finish the route before going to the repair location for a permanent repair.

Two caveats when creating your emergency repair kit:

- Focus on minor, easy-to-accomplish repairs that don't require expensive tools.

- Customize the emergency repair kit based on your equipment, technicians and experience.

- Consider technician skill when deciding what types of repairs he can perform. (Note: This falls under the rule, "Don't send your ducks to eagle school.") Be sure to train technicians when providing them with repair kits.

- Make sure technicians report what repairs they've made. When conducting truck inspections, check repair kits to see what parts are used. Track repairs to find problem areas. Modify repair kits based on what you find.

A few dollars and moments spent training technicians to make field repairs will pay dividends far exceeding the costs. Your customers and bottom line will benefit.

I. Back up critical spray equipment

If it's critical, back it up! Have you ever lost an important computer file you needed immediately? Everyone has experienced this situation. Hopefully, we learn from our mistakes and start backing up our critical files. Spray professionals have the same issue with their spray equipment. Companies rely heavily on spray equipment, yet in many cases, there's no backup. If a piece of equipment is critical to the business, then it's vital to have a backup.

It doesn't matter what the equipment is – truck, trailer, power sprayer, duster or compressed air sprayer – if the equipment is needed to do the job, keep a backup. Companies of all sizes, from owner/operator to huge national fleets, seem surprised when a key piece of equipment fails.

What happens when we don't have the spray equipment we need to complete our jobs?

➤ Missed and cancelled appointments
➤ Unhappy customers
➤ Lost revenue
➤ Employee downtime waiting for equipment and running around town trying to find a solution
➤ Overtime expenses
➤ Higher repair expenses.

Operating conditions that require backup equipment are:
> Equipment failure
> Equipment is down for maintenance
> Equipment is in the wrong location
> Equipment contains the wrong product (chemical)
> Equipment is on a vehicle that was in a traffic accident
> Equipment damage caused by technician misuse.

It gets worse. Equipment sometimes fails during the busy season, when the company can least afford downtime. This is also the time when the customer's pest or weed pressure is greatest, making them less willing to tolerate delays. The busy season is also when demand for repair services is greatest – there might be a delay replacing a part. Many vendors reduced inventory during the recession, which could extend the lead time on replacement parts.

So how do we solve this problem?

• **Identify critical equipment.** Review equipment by vehicle, service and technician to identify the most important tools.

• **Develop a backup plan for each critical item.** For some items, it might be easiest to buy a replacement. For more expensive items, be creative. Look through that pile of used equipment in the corner to see if you can create something valuable out of it. Keeping a trailer in reserve can be cheaper than keeping an extra vehicle in the fleet.

• **Review the plan.** Review the equipment backup plan annually to ensure it's still applicable. Test the backup equipment periodically to ensure it's functioning properly. Don't assume equipment sitting in the corner for years is still going to work.

Time spent identifying critical equipment and developing backup plans will save time, money and stress during the busy season.

J.   Prevent freeze damage

Additional risk for spray professionals comes during the winter. Deep freeze conditions can cause considerable damage to spray equipment. Some of the most expensive parts are most at risk of freeze damage. Water can freeze in lines, and ice can damage pumps, spray guns, line strainers (filters) and hand sprayers. In addition to the added cost of equipment repairs, customer appointments will be missed while equipment thaws out or is repaired. There are steps to take to reduce the risk of freeze damage to spray equipment.

Equipment design

Work with an equipment provider to build in preventive measures, such as installing a:

- Valve between tank and filter to shut off the flow of water through the system

- Drain at a low point in the system to allow water to drain out

- Fitting (like a tee or cross) with a removable plug to allow the addition of anti-freeze to the pump

Operations

- Train technicians to be aware of, and take steps to, prevent freeze damage. Remind techs damaged equipment affects their ability to provide outstanding service to customers and hinders the company financially.

- Train technicians to always release the pressure when they're done spraying. Systems under pressure will experience more damage from freezing than would otherwise. This is especially true for handheld compressed air sprayers and backpacks.

- Train technicians not to use frozen equipment until it thaws. Using or running frozen equipment will exacerbate small problems (i.e., more expensive problems, longer delays, etc.).

- Store vehicles in places where the equipment won't freeze.

Never underestimate the damage ice can do to equipment. Ice destroyed these heavy-duty brass ball valves.

- Wrap hoses with insulating material to reduce freeze risk.

- Cover equipment with insulating blankets at night.

- Purchase a pump heater to keep your pump warm and cozy at night.

- Build a pump heater by hanging a light bulb inside a cardboard box over your pump. Be sure there's no risk of fire.

- Drain water from equipment before an expected freeze.

- Add antifreeze to equipment stored for the winter.

- If storing a pest control sprayer for the winter, consider removing the pump to perform annual preventive maintenance.

Awareness and preparation are key to preventing freeze damage to your spray equipment. Remind technicians of their responsibilities to prevent damage to company equipment. Perform spot checks to ensure your policies are implemented. Track damage by technician to identify repeat offenders and equipment design problems.

K. Use spray equipment properly

A spray wand isn't a crowbar. This sounds obvious, but it's not. Ensure technicians are using equipment correctly. Many technicians seem to think a spray wand also serves to open cabinets and gates and move obstacles out of the way.

Using a spray wand this way will destroy it. Ensure employees are well trained on all equipment. Observe employees using equipment in the field. Companies that charge employees for damaged equipment have fewer problems than companies that are more lenient in this area.

L. Equipment inspections: Trust but verify

Many spray equipment repairs are preventable. These repairs cost spray professionals money that could be better spent elsewhere. To quote Ronald Reagan, "Self delusion in the face of unpleasant facts is folly."

Your company might have: the top of the line spray equipment, the best technicians, the best training program and procedure manual in the industry, and implemented the recommended preflight checklist. (See Appendix D.)

However, if you don't check on technicians periodically, you might be getting results you don't expect, which can impact customers and cost money.

Perform periodic truck inspections. Start with regular, frequent inspections and reduce frequency as the results of the inspections improve. Truck inspections of spray equipment can be scheduled or done by surprise. One of our customers inspects his truck biweekly before a technician can collect his paycheck. Another customer has one supervisor perform the equipment inspections, while another supervisor conducts monthly training meetings.

Just because you told a technician something was important during new hire training doesn't mean they're still doing it. If they see you're not following up or other technicians aren't following procedures, the technician will question why it needs to be done or find a shortcut that costs the company money.

Here's a brief checklist that can be completed in a couple of minutes:

Cleanliness
- ➤ Is there chemical buildup on the tank or in the truck bed?
- ➤ Is there debris or trash in the bed?
- ➤ Is the truck supporting your brand by being sparkling clean?

Leaks
- ➤ Are there any puddles in the truck?
- ➤ Is there water anywhere it's not supposed to be?
- ➤ Are there water or chemical stains to indicate leaks?
- ➤ Follow water from the tank through the spray gun to be sure you don't miss anything. Key risk areas are the tank fittings, pump, hose reel swivel and spray gun.

Inspect equipment regularly to identify problems before they become serious. Here the hose wore grooves in the camper shell.

Hoses
> ➢ Inspect hoses for structural integrity. There should be no cuts, punctures, scrapes, bandaids, excessive wear, etc.
> ➢ Inspect feeder hoses for kinks that prevent proper flow.
> ➢ Unroll and inspect the first 20 to 30 feet of spray hose. This is where most leaks occur.
> ➢ Are fittings and clamps in good condition?

Security
> ➢ Are tank bands intact and properly securing the tank?
> ➢ Are the toolboxes secure? Is there rust on the securing bolts?
> ➢ Are toolbox locks functioning properly?
> ➢ Are the hand tools secure?
> ➢ Is equipment securely attached to truck?

Safety
> ➢ Are sharp or jagged edges creating a hazard?
> ➢ Are hot engine components creating a burn hazard?
> ➢ Do moving parts have guards to prevent injury?
> ➢ Do hose reel lock functions properly?
> ➢ Is there any obvious damage or excessive wear on equipment? For example, are spray wands being used as crowbars? Is the engine pull cord frazzled?

If time allows, start the power equipment. Listen for normal operation, and check the pressure gauge for normal operating pressure. Perform a spray test by spraying material back into the tank. Check for normal operating ranges, then check spray pattern for completeness. This inspection should take no more than a few minutes per truck. The payback in reduced downtime, fewer missed appointments and lower pest control spray equipment repairs will be significant. You'll find coaching opportunities to provide feedback to technicians and equipment problems at the office, where they're much cheaper to fix than in the field. Consider rewarding technicians who consistently keep their equipment in excellent condition.

M. Policies and procedures

Additional policies and procedures to reduce downtime, missed appointments and equipment repair expense are:

- **Assign equipment to specific employees and hold them responsible.** Any piece of equipment assigned to an individual will have fewer problems and less downtime than equipment multiple employees use. Equipment left in a common area will be pillaged for parts so all that remains is junk. Assign equipment to one employee, and hold that employee responsible for ensuring the equipment is in sound condition. This doesn't necessarily mean the employee should make repairs. The employee is responsible for promptly calling equipment problems to management's attention. Companies that make employees pay for damaged equipment have fewer problems than companies that don't.

- **Track problems.** The old adage, "what gets meausured, gets done" applies to spray equipment. Track equipment problems to identify issues and causes. Track problems by vehicle, technician and component. If every technician has trouble with component C, the problem is component C. When equipment is repurchased, a solution other than component C should be pursued. If employee E is the only one having a problem with component C, perhaps employee E requires additional training. If component C works well on every vehicle except Truck T, perhaps Truck T has a wiring problem. Track problems and use the data to improve equipment selection and design, employee training, and company policies and procedures.

- **Train and retrain.** Ensure all new employees receive thorough training on all the equipment they'll be using. Periodically retrain all employees about the proper use of equipment. Don't let them tell you they know what they're doing. If that were the case, you wouldn't be spending as much money fixing equipment. Just because you showed employee E on day one how you wanted the equipment used, doesn't mean employee E is still doing what you want. He has probably found a shortcut, which probably costs the company money.

- **Develop good policies and procedures.** Good policies and procedures for spray equipment will boost productivity and reduce downtime. Document your equipment policies in writing, and review them periodically with employees. Continuously update and improve company policies.

- **Supervisor ride alongs.** Supervisors should periodically ride along with employees to see how they're doing their job, how the equipment functions and how the equipment layout in the truck is working. Without actually pulling hose, supervisors don't know how employees are doing or how the equipment is helping or hurting productivity.

- **Continuously improve equipment.** Never be satisfied with your spray equipment. Keep looking for improvements and new ideas to help the company perform better.

Sources of new ideas are:

- **Ask technicians** for ideas and advice about improving equipment. Employees use this equipment every day. They're an ideal source of ideas.

- **Steal ideas.** Industry meetings are a great place for new ideas. Talk to colleagues and competitors to find out what works for them. Walk the parking lot at these meetings, and take photos of competitor's trucks to get new ideas.

- **Discuss equipment and safety at staff meetings.** If you don't discuss it, employees might assume it doesn't matter to the company, and you could miss out on good ideas.

- **Equipment vendor.** Your equipment vendor is a great source of ideas for improvements. He sees many different equipment ideas. Because you've concentrated your equipment purchases with a trusted vendor, he'll be more than happy to assist you.

- **Track ideas and suggestions for improvement.** Track all ideas and suggestions so when it's time to purchase new equipment, you haven't forgotten anything.

Calibration

- It's not the goal of this book to explain calibration training. It's important to calibrate and recalibrate your spray equipment. There are many resources available on the Internet about this topic. The key point is calibration is set for a specific piece of equipment under specific settings and conditions. If anything changes, recalibrate.

Make use of slow periods

- Use slow periods for preventive maintenance and retraining. See the year-end checklist Appendix A.

APPENDIX

A. Top five year-end equipment tips

Spray professionals should use the slower time at the end of the year to ensure their equipment is in tip-top shape for the coming year. These tasks need to be done anyway, so do them when business is slow and when they won't negatively impact your customers and schedule.

- **Inspections.** Use slow periods to perform thorough inspections of vehicles and power, hand and backpack sprayers. Is everything clean, in the proper place and in proper working order?

- **Clean it out.** Run clean water through power, hand and backpack sprayers to prevent chemical buildup. Inspect and clean out spray tanks. Thoroughly clean filters and replace bad filter screens if necessary.

- **Winterize it.** The best way to prevent freeze damage is to ensure your sprayer equipment isn't exposed to freezing temperatures. If you can't do that, do the next best thing: Get as much water as possible out of the sprayers. Use a compressor to blow the air out of the hoses. Open all valves. Remove filters, spray guns and anything else you can to prevent freeze damage. Run a little antifreeze through the system. The pump on a power sprayer is the greatest risk; remove it and store indoors if possible. If not, hang a utility light over the spray pump or wrap it with an electric battery warmer to prevent freezing. Never put anything hot on a frozen pump in an attempt to defrost it. It won't work, and you might destroy the pump. Starting or using frozen equipment will result in expensive damage.

- **Preventive maintenance.** Slow periods are an ideal time for preventive maintenance. Because of hard use and harsh chemicals, all spray equipment needs maintenance. Don't wait for equipment to break or wear out. Service it now so you don't have downtime and missed appointments during the busy season.

- **Training.** Train during slow periods. Truck and equipment inspections will identify training opportunities. It's important to remember just because you trained Employee E on day one doesn't mean he's still doing it the way you want him to do it. You can never do too much safety training.

B. Top 10 spray equipment productivity tips

1. **Check and clean the filter.** There's nothing you can do with spray equipment that will save you more money than this simple activity. Clogged filters can starve the pump. Damaged or missing filters allow debris to damage and clog the sprayer. We repair and replace more sprayers because of clogged or missing filters than any other reason.

2. **Release the pressure.** After spraying, release the pressure by squeezing the handle of your spray equipment to release system pressure. If you don't want to waste the material, spray it back into the tank. The equipment will have fewer breakdowns and last longer if you remove the stress of constant pressure from the spray components. Never store equipment under pressure overnight.

3. **Don't use higher pressure than you need.** Don't push equipment to its limits. Because techs run power spray rigs at high speeds to complete jobs quickly they tend to overpressurize B&G and backpack sprayers. These actions reduce sprayer life. A power spray rig can run at extremes for short periods, but it's not designed to be run full capacity all the time. Running in the red for an extended period of time will shorten engine and pump life. Make sure operators know proper operating ranges.

4. **Clean it out.** Periodically rinse the system with clean water to remove old chemical buildup and debris. Chemical buildup and debris can clog a filter, starve a pump, damage spray tips, and wreak havoc on other components. So when in doubt, rinse it out. Follow all labels and laws when cleaning spray tanks.

5. **Don't wait for failure – perform preventive maintenance (PM).** PM will save time, money, equipment breakdowns and unhappy customers. Because equipment is running hard and pumping harsh chemicals, it will need service, which is cheaper and less painful if you do it before you need it. Read manufacturer's recommendations, then customize them for the particular use and application. A sound preventive maintenance program is your best friend for reducing equipment down time and improving productivity.

6. **Don't ignore problems – deal with them promptly.** We're constantly amazed at the equipment problems spray techs tolerate. They'll continue to use leaking pumps, hose and backpacks. Spray equipment problems always worsen and become more expensive to fix. Encourage employees to report problems promptly so you can take the appropriate action.

7. **Emergency repair kits.** Many simple repairs can be performed in the field. These repairs allow technicians to finish their work before heading to the service site for more thorough repairs. Assess technicians' skill and training to determine which parts you're comfortable with them changing in the field. Tracking can go a long way toward understanding the causes of breakdowns. Track equipment failures by part to determine which items to stock on trucks. Also, track equipment failures by technician to identify training opportunities and failures by truck to set times for preventive maintenance and replacement.

8. **Preflight checklist.** Every pilot has a checklist and goes through a preflight routine before he flies. Spray

techs should do the same. Before heading to the first stop, a few minutes spent checking equipment can save time and money, and prevent downtime that hinders timely service to customers. Here's the key point. If there's an equipment problem, you're probably better off knowing about it at the office than in the field, where most likely it will take longer and cost more to fix. Technicians should report problems or exceptions to their supervisor.

9. **Training and retraining.** Ensure any technician using a sprayer thoroughly understands how to use it. Supervisors should observe a technician's operating procedures and check equipment operating pressure and filter. Provide periodic retraining. Train operators to listen and observe sprayers so they can identify problems.

10. **Avoid freeze damage.** Never expose sprayers to freezing temperatures. Water freezing in sprayers will burst pumps, filters, valves, fittings and spray guns.

C. Quality spray tips

- **No. 1. Buying a new power sprayer.** Common mistakes to avoid:
  - ➢ Buying equipment without planning exactly what you need
  - ➢ Not asking for help or advice
  - ➢ Buying one sprayer for every possible application
  - ➢ Buying what the salesman is selling instead of what you need
  - ➢ Buying solely on price
  - ➢ Not knowing what you're getting (even the little parts matter)

Questions to ask before buying
  - ➢ What's the main job (80 percent) of this sprayer?
  - ➢ What's the warranty?
  - ➢ What parts are likely to fail, and where do I buy replacement parts?
  - ➢ What maintenance is needed, and how do I do it?
  - ➢ What will it be like once the sprayer is in the vehicle, and how easy will it be for a technician to use the sprayer?
  - ➢ Will there be room for storage (toolboxes)?
  - ➢ Is the sprayer easy to clean?
  - ➢ Is the sprayer easy to service?
  - ➢ Is this the sprayer with which I want to standardize the fleet?
  - ➢ If a leak develops, how does it shut off?

- **No. 2. Tank tips.** When buying a new tank:
  - ➢ Determine what size tank you need based on the number of jobs per day and number of gallons per job.

Tank size
> ➤ Too big creates problems for the vehicle (stopping, control, repairs).
> ➤ Too small will kill productivity by stopping to refill.
> ➤ It's better to fill a 100-gallon tank halfway than to have to fill a 50-gallon tank twice a day.
> ➤ Make sure there's a shut off valve right after the tank fitting so you can shut off the water flow if there's a problem (for bottom feed tanks).
> ➤ Make sure it's easy to open the lid and put chemicals into the tank.

Tank maintenance tips
> ➤ You must clean the tank periodically to prevent chemical buildup and debris from entering the sprayer.
> ➤ Periodically check that the tank is secured (straps, bolts).

• **No. 3. Spray hose tips.** When buying new hose:
> ➤ It's better to buy too much hose than not enough.
> ➤ Smaller diameter is lighter and cheaper. Buy the smallest diameter that will allow you to do your job.

Spray hose use and maintenance

> ➤ Run the hose through a rag when rolling it back onto the reel to remove debris that could damage the hose
> ➤ Inspect your hose for damage, excessive wear and leaks.
> ➤ When the first few feet of hose start showing wear, it's much cheaper to cut off a few feet of hose than to miss appointments for a hose repair. Cut off the first few feet of hose before it leaks.
> ➤ Unroll all hose off the hose reel periodically, then power up the system and roll the hose back onto the

reel. This helps prevent the hose from flattening and causing pressure-related problems.

➢ Periodically reverse the hose. Remove the spray gun and attach the outside end of the hose to the reel. Put your spray gun back on the other end. This will even out the wear and extend hose life.

➢ Keep a hose repair kit on the vehicle so you can make minor hose repairs in the field.

- **No. 4. Hose reel tips.** When buying a new reel:

  ➢ Buy a quality, name brand reel. Cheap reels won't withstand hard use.

  ➢ Ask where and when replacement parts are available.

  ➢ Buy a swivel repair kit. Be prepared for the swivel to leak.

  ➢ Electric reels can be worth the additional cost by making the tech's job easier.

  ➢ Make sure the reel is easily accessible for use and maintenance when you install it.

  ➢ Don't hang extra plumbing on the swivel because it will shorten swivel O-ring life and cause it to leak much sooner.

Hose reel use and maintenance
  ➢ Pay attention to the swivel. The O-rings will leak eventually. Be prepared.

- **No. 5. Spray pump tips.** When buying a new sprayer pump:

Be sure you're buying the right pump for the job:
  ➢ Volume (GPM)
  ➢ Pressure (PSI)
  ➢ Match pump to tank size and hose size/length
  ➢ Match pump to material being applied
  ➢ Match pump to the job (e.g., will pump be used

hard eight to 10 hours a day?)
> Are replacement parts readily available?
> Be sure there's a shut-off valve in front of the pump so the pump can be removed for service even if the tank is full.

Sprayer pump use and maintenance
> Perform preventive maintenance during slow periods. Don't wait for pump to fail.
> Know the pump warning signs. At first sign of a problem, investigate.
> If the pump sounds or looks differently than usual, or output is different than normal, investigate.
> If you think there's a problem with the pump, it's probably best not to keep using it.
> Be sure there's effective filtration in front of the pump.
> Running the pump at full speed all the time will reduce pump life.

- **No. 6. Manual sprayers - backpack and hand.** When buying a new manual sprayer:
  > Standardize. Buy all the same manufacturer or model.
  > Buy quality. Pay particular attention to the pump mechanism and spray valve (gun).

Make sure:
> It's comfortable to wear/carry.
> It's easy to service and clean the filter.
> Replacement parts are readily available.
> Multiple spray tips can be used with the sprayer.

When using a manual sprayer
> Inspect and test it before starting a route.
> Make sure the sprayer is secure in the truck to prevent damage and accidents.
> Check and clean the filter regularly.

➢ Don't overpressure it.

➢ Release the pressure after every stop.

➢ Prevent freezing.

➢ Clean it out periodically.

➢ Perform regular preventive maintenance.

➢ To reduce downtime, keep an emergency repair kit of easy-to-replace parts on the vehicle.

• **No. 7. Spray equipment.** General guidelines for selection, use and maintenance:

Selection

➢ **Standardize.** Standardizing equipment makes, training, maintenance and parts inventory easier. Companies that don't standardize end up with piles of junk.

➢ **Buy quality equipment.** Cheap equipment doesn't last.

➢ **Smart design.** Equipment should be easy to use, easy to clean and maintain, and comfortable to use.

➢ **The right product for the job.** Be sure the equipment is properly sized for the size and number of jobs.

➢ **Availability of replacement parts.** If replacement parts aren't readily available, the equipment is disposable.

➢ **Availability of options.** Options, such as multiple tips, increase equipment usefulness.

Use

➢ Secure it to prevent damage and injury. Be sure equipment is secured in the vehicle before driving off.

➢ Inspect the equipment at the office before driving off to the first job.

➢ Train technicians to to use equipment properly to prevent problems.

➢ Release pressure after each stop.

➢ Run equipment at the appropriate speed and pressure.

➢ Take the appropriate steps to prevent freeze damage.

> Train techs to report problems rather than live with them.

Maintenance

Technician
> Clean the filter to prevent problems and reduce downtime.
> Clean the tank and equipment to remove debris and prevent clogging.
> Clean and replace tips by using a gentle soap and old toothbrush. Replace tips annually.
> Carry an emergency repair kit to keep critical parts on the vehicle.
> Periodic calibration is essential to good results. Recalibrate regularly or when conditions change.

Management
> Preventive maintenance during slow periods saves money and reduces downtime.
> Supervisors should inspect equipment to ensure policy compliance and identify problems.
> Just because you trained a tech once, doesn't mean he's still trained. Retrain him.
> Assign equipment to one person. When one person is responsible, equipment lasts longer.
> Encourage techs to report problems, but don't kill the messenger. Encourage problem reporting.
> Track problems by equipment, technician and vehicle to identify problem areas and opportunities.

D. Preflight checklist

PCO Preflight Checklist

Identify problems early, where and when you can more easily deal with them.

HAND SPRAYERS
- [ ] Puddle under sprayer?
- [ ] Visual inspection.
- [ ] Pressure test.
- [ ] Spray test for leaks, pattern, etc.

TANK
- [ ] Check for leaks, especially around fittings
- [ ] Check that tank is secure.
- [ ] Check for debris.
- [ ] Lid present and secure?

LINE STRAINER/FILTER
- [ ] Open and clean out debris in screen.
- [ ] Check O-ring for swelling.

GAS ENGINE
- [ ] Gas/oil properly filled?
- [ ] Gas cap secure?
- [ ] Oil leaks?
- [ ] Check belt for wear/snugness.
- [ ] Check pull cord for excessive wear.
- [ ] Check recoil for proper rewind action.

PUMP
- [ ] Staining or evidence of leaks?
- [ ] Visible leaks?
- [ ] Pump specific problems, such as:
      diaphragm pump oil reservoir contamination?

SUPPLY/FEEDER HOSES
- [ ] Leaks?
- [ ] Excessive wear or bubbling?
- [ ] Kinks?
- [ ] Fittings in good condition?
- [ ] Clamps snug/hoses secure?

HOSE REEL/SPRAY HOSE
- [ ] Puddle under reel/hose/gun?
- [ ] Reel lock operational?
- [ ] Reel turns properly?
- [ ] Unwind 20-30 feet of hose.
- [ ] Inspect hose for excessive wear.

PRESSURE TEST
- [ ] Start up power sprayer.
- [ ] Check for abnormal sounds.
- [ ] Check entire system for leaks.
- [ ] Electric pump:
  - [ ] Evidence of power to pump.
- [ ] Gas Pump:
  - [ ] Belts/pulleys aligned.
  - [ ] Belts/pulleys turn OK.

SPRAY TEST
- [ ] Test gun by spraying back into tank.
- [ ] Pressure OK?
- [ ] Flow rate OK?
- [ ] Spray pattern OK?
- [ ] Rewind hose (manual/electric) to ensure
      proper reel operation.

**INSPECT OTHER SPECIALIZED or
CUSTOM EQUIPMENT**
- [ ] Proper operation.
- [ ] No leaks.
- [ ] Load security.

QUALITY
Equipment & Spray
Our Equipment. Your Success.

For more information visit:
- [ ] www.Qspray.com

Or contact us at:
- [ ] info@Qspray.com
- [ ] 800.675.7485

DEFINITIONS

Here are definitions for some of the equipment commonly referred to in this book.

Spray equipment. Manual or powered equipment designed to apply a product, usually water or oil based, onto a target by putting the product under pressure and expelling it through a nozzle.

Spray technician/spray tech. A person who uses spray equipment to apply a product.

Manual sprayers. Sprayers powered by a technician's efforts (usually by pumping) rather than a power source such as a battery or gas motor. Manual sprayer usually describes hand, compressed air and backpack sprayers. Usually, manual sprayers are bought off the shelf, and there are few options or customization available.

Hand sprayers or compressed air sprayers. Small sprayers, usually no more than three gallons, that rely on a spray tech's muscle power to pump them up. The pump mechanism fills the tank with compressed air, which expels the product when the spray valve is opened.

Backpack or knapsack sprayers. Sprayers, manual or power, that a technician carries on his back.

Power sprayers. Sprayers powered by a source other than a technician. For our purposes, the power source is usually a small gas or electric engine. Power sprayers often contain a tank, pump, motor, hose and reel, and spray gun. There are innumerable variations, options and configurations.

Pump. A mechanical device that transfers or delivers fluids (or dusts).

Motor or engine. The power source that drives a pump. Usually motors on spray equipment are electric or gas powered. Some agricultural uses are PTO, power take off, which derives power from the drive shaft of the vehicle.

Tank or water tank. A container that holds the water and product (chemical) to be applied by the sprayer. It's usually made from plastic, fiberglass, steel or aluminum.

Hose reel. A device that holds the spray hose. Usually, the spray hose wraps around the central drum of the hose reel to efficiently store the spray hose. Hose reels are manual or electric-motor rewind.

Spray hose. A flexible tube for conveying liquids. For spray equipment, the spray hose enables a technician to move the product from the tank to where it needs to be applied. On manual sprayers, the hose is usually 3- to 4-feet long. On power sprayers, the hose can be as long as 400 feet.

Spray gun. An apparatus resembling a gun used to apply a product, in the form of a spray, to the target. A more accurate description is a spray valve, but this term isn't used commonly.

Spray tip. A spray nozzle installed on the end of a spray gun used to disperse liquid into a spray. There's a wide variety of nozzles available for every use and purpose. Nozzle characteristics are material (such as brass, plastic or stainless steel), flow rate (in gallons per minute) and pattern (such as cone, stream or flat fan and droplet size.

Valves. They open, close or regulate the flow of liquid through the sprayer. Most commonly used valves on power sprayers are gate, ball and check. Valves are usually made from brass, steel or plastic.

Quick disconnect (QD). Quick disconnects are fittings, usually made of brass or steel, that allow a spray component, e.g., a spray gun, to be removed easily without tools. QDs make it easy for spray techs to change spray guns or remove them for storage or service.

ACKNOWLEDGEMENTS

A few people must be thanked for their support, love, friendship and contributions. First, my wonderful wife, Wendy, who has stuck by me for 25 years and supported all my harebrained schemes. Thanks to the team at Quality Equipment and Spray that provided the learning that went into this book: Ken Brutsman, Steve Costa, Amanda Kalwa and Rob Holmes. They're the best spray equipment team in the nation, and without them, this book wouldn't exist. Thanks to my friend, Arthur P. Mullin, the most generous person I've met. And lastly, many thanks to the wonderful folks at *Pest Management Professional* magazine, who didn't laugh when I proposed the idea of a pest control equipment column and have helped and supported me for many years.